**Legend**

Boundary of Yugoslavia
Other international boundaries
Boundaries of the six Republics
Boundaries of the Autonomous Provinces

0    M i l e s    80

R O U M A N I A

Belgrade

Bucharest

44°

Bor

Kragujevac

R. Morava

R. Danube

E R B I A

Niš

Kosovo

Sofia

(Košmet)

B U L G A R I A

42°

Skopje

M A C E D O N I A

R. Vardar

Mavrovo

E

Lake Ohrid

Lake Prespa

G

E A N

S E A

40°

20°    22°    24°

THE MODERN WORLD
GENERAL EDITOR: C. H. C. BLOUNT

# YUGOSLAVIA

BY
A. W. PALMER

OXFORD UNIVERSITY PRESS
1964

*Oxford University Press, Amen House, London E.C.4*

GLASGOW  NEW YORK  TORONTO  MELBOURNE  WELLINGTON
BOMBAY  CALCUTTA  MADRAS  KARACHI  LAHORE  DACCA
CAPE TOWN  SALISBURY  NAIROBI  IBADAN  ACCRA
KUALA LUMPUR  HONG KONG

PRINTED  IN  GREAT  BRITAIN  BY
NORTHUMBERLAND  PRESS  LIMITED
GATESHEAD  ON  TYNE

# CONTENTS

3

# LIST OF PLATES

## LIST OF FIGURES

Illustrations are reproduced by courtesy of the Information Bureau of Yugoslavia: Plates 1a, 2a, 3a, 4b, 5a, 5b, 7, 8a, 8b, 8c, 8d; Yugoslavia National Tourist Office: Plates 1b, 2b, 3b, 4a; Imperial War Museum: Plate 6; Cas Oorthuys: the cover photograph.

# A NOTE ON PRONUNCIATION

'Dj' in Yugoslav names is pronounced roughly as the 'du' in 'endurance'; 'lj' as the 'lli' in 'brilliant'; 'ić' as 'itch'; 'č' as 'ch' in 'church'; 'š' as 'sh' in 'sheep'; 'ž' as 's' in 'leisure'; 'dž' as 'J' in 'Jack'. Vowels: 'a' as in 'last'; 'i' as 'ee' in 'keep'; 'o' is pronounced between the 'o' in 'top' and the 'aw' in 'awful'. Other letters are pronounced, more or less, as in English.

N.B. 'Croat' in English has two syllables, although the word used for Croat in Yugoslavia (*Hrvat*) has only one.

# I

## THE COUNTRY AND THE PEOPLES

A TRAVELLER WHO crosses over to Belgium and takes a trans-continental express from Ostend, finds himself by midnight rumbling across Western Germany, with occasional glimpses of the River Rhine and its castles in the moonlight. Next morning, still in Germany, he crosses a small river, the Danube beginning its 1,700 mile passage down to the Black Sea. His train enters Austria and spends the afternoon in a winding journey through the Alps. Eventually it passes into one last tunnel, under the peaks of the Karawanken, and emerges at another frontier-station, Jesenice. It is just twenty-four hours since the train left Ostend. Few travellers receive a favourable impression of Jesenice, for its line in factory chimneys is distinctly drab; many are impatient to press on to the Adriatic coast or Greece, and feel irritated at a delay of (nominally) half an hour. But while the express waits for completion of the wearisome Customs' formalities, there is time for the traveller to observe one or two strange features around him. He may notice that one of the factory chimneys has an illuminated red star on it; or that the name of the station is written twice, first in familiar characters and beneath it in what looks like Russian and is, in fact, the Russian-type alphabet, called Cyrillic; or that on the wall of a waiting-room there is a portrait of a military leader—an immaculate uniform, a square face, alert eyes, and a firm mouth. And, seeing all this, the traveller would realize that he was, indeed, in Yugoslavia. The Cyrillic writing gives the place-names in Serbian, the red

7

star reminds the visitor that he is in a communist state (although not, it should be added, a Russian-dominated one) and the subject of the portrait is the Yugoslav President, Marshal Tito.

Most of the countries of the modern world have names that go far back into history. In this respect, as in much else, Yugoslavia is an exception: it is a creation of the twentieth century, existing in practice only since 1918 and as the official title of the country only since 1929. The present political form of Yugoslavia—a Federation of six 'People's Republics'—is even more recent; it dates only from 1946. At the opening of this century three-quarters of the Yugoslav lands were still within the Austro-Hungarian or Turkish Empires. There can be few countries more 'modern'. And yet, wherever one travels through the ninety-nine thousand square miles that comprise the Federation, there is striking evidence of the past. There is nothing unusual in that; every land has its ruined castles and ancient churches, its proud cities preserving the splendour of an age that has been outpaced. Yugoslavia is unique in possessing relics that form a living testimony to the past of Europe as a whole, and not merely the history of any one ancient state. For Yugoslavia is one of those rare regions in the world where rival political, religious, and cultural traditions have met over the centuries. To some extent the real frontiers of Yugoslavia still run through the country rather than round it.

Nothing illustrates so vividly the rich variety of the Yugoslav heritage as a comparison of some of the leading towns. Each has a distinctive character of its own. There are five cities with a population of more than 150,000. In order of size they are Belgrade (the federal capital), Zagreb, Sarajevo, Skopje, and Ljubljana. Belgrade is a natural guard-post that has sprung up around a limestone crag, some 140 feet high, commanding the meeting point of two great rivers, the Danube and the Sava. On the summit of the crag stands a fortress, the Kalemegdan, built by the Turks on Roman foundations and looking out over the wide plains beyond the rivers. In the last century and a half Belgrade has been taken and re-taken by invading armies no less than ten times. It is the chief city of the Serbian people and nowadays the administrative centre of the Serbian Republic; its churches belong to the Orthodox branch of Christianity, similar to the churches of modern Greece and of old pre-revolutionary Russia. Zagreb is two hundred and seventy miles to the northwest of Belgrade; it is the capital of Croatia, and the seat of a university with a distinguished record of scholarship. There the churches are Roman Catholic and, although Zagreb is today a thriving commercial centre, the visitor can still see a gateway of the old mediaeval city to remind him that it once served as an outpost of Catholic culture on the fringe of a barbarian world. From Zagreb he can catch an overnight train to Sarajevo, three hundred miles to the south and the capital of Bosnia-Herzegovina. In the morning he will emerge from a ferro-concrete station to a city still dominated by mosques, for even now Sarajevo is second only to Istanbul among the Muslim towns of Europe. Yet it also possesses an Orthodox cathedral and a Roman Catholic cathedral and, until the German invaders swept on the city in 1941, there was a large and ancient Jewish community as well. Skopje, the capital of Macedonia, is not as cosmopolitan as Sarajevo, but there too, until the tragic earthquake of 1963, mosques and minarets continued to recall five centuries of Turkish power. Skopje is indeed nearer to Istanbul, the old capital of Turkey, than it is to the last of the five cities, Ljubljana. For Ljubljana is the centre of Yugoslavia's most northern republic, Slovenia, and is 650 miles away, further than from Inverness to Dover. Ljubljana (the name means 'well-beloved') has all the charm of an Austrian provincial city—as, of course, it used to be. There is an old castle on a rocky hill, a fast-flowing stream cutting its way between baroque churches and an old university, and a backcloth of mountain-peaks, snow-capped for much of the year. Add to this catalogue of the five largest towns Yugoslavia's oldest port, Split, which has grown up around a Roman Emperor's palace; and Dubrovnik, a walled-city permanently influenced by its long rivalry with Venice; and you will see that Yugoslavia is as diversified a land as any in Europe.

The peoples are as varied as the cities. The Slovenes, in the north, are hard-working and thorough-going, neat and tidy; they look at the invasion of political affairs into their lives with a certain resignation. They do not actually despise their more excitable fellow-countrymen from the south; they merely seek to remain aloof from their outbursts of temperamental violence. Nevertheless, the Slovenes are true and loyal Yugoslavs; in the Second World War no town in the country had so many of its inhabitants sent to concentration camps by the enemy as Ljubljana. The Croats, who are the Slovenes' southern neighbours, have the greatest variety of landscape in their boomerang-shaped republic—the broad plains of Slavonia, rolling hill country covered with vineyards, forests in which the villagers still hunt wolves in winter, bare mountains, and the magnificent coastline of Dalmatia. It is difficult to generalize about the Croat character; for what do a steel-worker in Zagreb and a shepherd-boy on the Velebit Mountains share in common? A rare capacity for talk, perhaps; a fondness for tinkering with machinery in a disarmingly optimistic spirit;

and a natural adventurousness that has led Croats to emigrate on a bigger scale than other Yugoslavs. This last characteristic has contributed to the curious circumstance that there are now more people of Croatian descent living in the cities of the U.S.A. than in the cities of Croatia itself. (Significantly, the largest concentration of American Croats is in the motor-car industry of Detroit.) Yet, despite this spirit of overseas enterprise, the Croats have shown over the centuries that they possess an intensive patriotism. At its best this patriotism has inspired noble works of art (one remembers in particular the titanic figure of the tenth-century Bishop Gregory, whom the great Dalmatian sculptor, Meštrović, has shown defying Croatia's enemies in Split). At its worst Croatian patriotism is debased into a narrowly regional fanaticism violently opposed to the whole idea of an all-Yugoslav state.

While the Croats and Slovenes are essentially Central European, the other Yugoslav peoples are as Eastern European as the mountains and rivers which have so largely dominated their existence. The Macedonians, in the far south, are the most backward and until recently were content to live in an oxen-powered pastoral society. The inhabitants of Bosnia-Herzegovina are not a separate nationality; they have inherited many of their habits from their former oppressors, the Turks, but they have remained racially Slavonic and prefer to describe themselves as Serbs (or, in the north, Croats) rather than 'Bosnians'. Life has been hard for them in their wild and mountainous country. And it has been no easier for their neighbours, the Montenegrins, a proud warrior people, physically taller than the other Yugoslavs, dark and sharp-featured. For five hundred years they fought against the Turks. When a son was born to a Montenegrin family, the villagers would offer a solemn prayer, 'May God grant that he never dies in bed.' Today there are less than half a million genuine Montenegrins, and the passions and blood-feuds belong to the past.

If the Montenegrins are numerically the smallest group of Yugoslavs, their close kinsfolk the Serbs are the largest. Serbs tend to be vigorous, exuberant, and gloriously unsystematic. Their traditional round dance, the Serbian *Kolo,* shows all these characteristics, with, sometimes, a hundred people linking themselves together in a long, wavering line for a frenzy of rejoicing. Serbia is a land of gentle hills and sad plains, a vista of dust-green crops broken by white farming settlements or new factories and, suddenly and surprisingly, a cluster of domes on some hillock where an ancient monastery recalls the grandeur of the country's mediaeval culture. Earlier this century the Serbs were perhaps too conscious of this largely legendary past, but more recent events have created new legends for them, less narrowly Serbian than the old. Conditions in Serbia are changing more markedly than further north. The Serbs are still dependent on the soil, but maize and pigs and horses play less part in their lives than they did even thirty years ago; to an increasing extent (and this is equally true of Bosnia), it is the mineral wealth beneath the surface that matters.

There is a 'People's Republic' for each of the six groups we have mentioned. Four of the republics— Slovenia, Croatia, Serbia, Macedonia—lie along the main trunk route from western Europe to the East. The other two republics—Bosnia-Herzegovina and Montenegro— lie to the west of this route. None of these republics is, of course, totally independent. The Yugoslav Federal Government in Belgrade decides all major questions of policy. Each of the six republics does, however, possess its own political assembly and a government which is responsible for purely local affairs (including education) and which frames an economic policy within the general pattern of development. There is thus some parallel between the function of a 'People's Republic' within Yugoslavia and that of a State within the U.S.A., although there are none of America's local variations in the law. In the Serbian People's Republic there are two 'Autonomous Provinces': the Voivodina in the north, where most of the people are not racially Serbs but are of Hungarian descent; and Kosovo-Metohija in the south, where there are many Albanians or, as they are called locally, 'Shqiptars'. The autonomous provinces have additional rights of self-government of their own, particularly concerning the use of locally-spoken languages. Kosovo-Metohija is commonly abbreviated to 'Kosmet' and we shall use this form when we refer to the province in later chapters.

The six People's Republics are not artificial creations, with boundaries drawn mainly for administrative convenience; as we have seen, they represent distinctive regions with traditions and histories of their own. One of the prime problems of any Yugoslav Government must be to harness the strength that comes from this diversity. Some foreign observers have regarded the existence of a Yugoslav State which comprises so many nationalities, cultures, and religions as a defiance of the common-sense of history. This is a superficial view. Although there remain many differences between the various peoples, there are certain features common to all; and each year that passes is emphasizing these aspects at the expense of the older ways.

Three main forces have bound, or are binding, the

nation together. The first of these is racial. The name 'Yugoslav' means 'the land of the South Slavs'. Now although we can find men and women of Italian or Hungarian or Roumanian or Albanian descent in Yugoslavia, 82 per cent. of the population are 'South Slavs'. This means that although their local loyalty may be to Serbia or Croatia or Montenegro, they are all members of the same race, just as Prussians and Bavarians are in Germany, or Neapolitans and Venetians in Italy. Moreover, the Yugoslavs are distant kinsfolk of the greatest of Slav nations, the Russians (and, for that matter, of the western Slavs, i.e. the Poles, the Czechs, and the Slovaks). This sense of kinship with Russia has been a powerful influence on the political and cultural development of the Yugoslavs in the last century and a half. But the feeling of common origin has not been strong enough to prevent feuds within the Slav family of nations. One of the most bitter of these has been waged between the Serbs and their eastern neighbours, the Bulgars, who are themselves a South Slav people. Early enthusiasts for Yugoslav union even hoped that the Bulgars would join the Serbs, Croats, and Slovenes in a Great South Slav confederation, but this was no more than a dream. Serbs and Bulgars became intensely suspicious of one another; their rivalry led them to fight each other on four occasions between 1885 and 1945. Bulgaria has remained an independent state and there seems little likelihood that it will ever enter a South Slav union. But all the other members of the South Slav race are bound together within the framework of the present federation.

The second influence that has brought the Yugoslavs together is resistance to outside oppression. Originally, as we shall see, this took the form of action against either

Austria or Turkey, the two great multi-national empires which between them dominated central and south-eastern Europe in the eighteenth and nineteenth centuries. During the First World War groups of Croats and Slovenes who had escaped from Austria-Hungary joined the Serbs (who were fighting valiantly on the same side as the British and French) in inducing the Allies to accept the right of all Yugoslavs to determine their political future once the war was over. It was under these conditions that the First Yugoslavia was created in 1918, with the King of Serbia ruling over what was officially called 'the Kingdom of the Serbs, Croats, and Slovenes'. But in 1941 this Yugoslav Kingdom collapsed after less than a fortnight's fighting against the Germans and their allies. Any defeated country that is occupied by enemies has to endure suffering. Few, however, have experienced such horrors as the South Slav lands, for after invasion came a civil war in which the cruelty of local fanatics shocked even the occupying authorities. Men and women realized that only joint action by all the peoples against the invaders and their hirelings could rid the country of this new reign of frightfulness. The population of Yugoslavia was literally decimated during the war; 1,700,000 people perished in the four years of bloodshed. The Second Yugoslavia, the present Federation, was born out of this experience. It is important to remember that even today, twenty years after these events, the monuments to the resistance which the traveller sees throughout the country have a direct impact which it is hard for those of us who have not lived in a ravaged land to appreciate. A pupil who enters his school each morning by passing a memorial which commemorates 200 'old boys' who were taken from their classes and, with their schoolmasters, shot as hostages is unlikely to forget his country's recent history. There is such a school in the Serbian town of Kragujevac.

It was the Second World War that led to the triumph of the third unifying force. When the First Yugoslavia was created there were ten main political parties, but each of them had a regional or narrowly religious basis. They tended to work against the newly unified state rather than for it, since each political group wished the part of the country in which it was strongest to dominate the rest. Only the small and recently-formed Communist Party had an all-Yugoslav structure, since it was based not on race or religion, but on class. In 1921 the Communist Party was declared illegal after one of its members had murdered the Minister of the Interior, but it survived as an underground organization, and more and more young intellectuals secretly joined the movement. Many of these recruits were not members of the working-class, and indeed had only a passing acquaintance with the writings of Karl Marx and other left-wing prophets. They became communists out of protest and disillusionment at the conditions around them; and they made Yugoslav communism far more independent in character than the communism of other countries. These were the men whom the Second World War brought to power. The Second Yugoslavia became a one-party communist state—and in the last chapter we shall have to consider the limitations that, to Western eyes, this communist dictatorship has imposed on political development—but we must remember that the 'League of Communists', as the Party is now called, is at all events a specifically Yugoslav organization, representative of the Federation as a whole and not of the regions which comprise it.

Nothing has yet been said of language; and when one

remembers the part that a common tongue has played in the unification of other countries, this omission may seem surprising. The difficulty is that there has never been such a language as 'Yugoslavian'. Some eleven hundred years ago, when the South Slavs were a wandering people invading the Balkans, they probably communicated with each other in the same form of speech. But as they settled in isolated villages or in regions separated from each other by formidable mountains, local peculiarities emerged. It was not until the end of the eighteenth century that a group of scholars evolved a method of turning one of the dialects spoken in Serbia and parts of Dalmatia into a written literary language, acceptable to all other Serbs. In the first half of the nineteenth century Croatian scholars succeeded in combining one of their dialects with Serbian, even though the Croats used (and still use) the Latin alphabet of western Europe and the Serbs used (and still use) the Cyrillic alphabet of eastern Europe. Thus there emerged 'Serbo-Croat', the main language of Yugoslavia, used, for example, on the currency and postage stamps. There are minor differences between Serbian and Croatian, not unlike the variations between English and American. The Serbs would see a film at a *bioskop*, while Croats would go to a *kino*; and the Croats tend to use the beautifully poetic *listopad* ('the falling of the leaf') to describe the month that the Serbs call, more prosaically, *oktobar*. In print the Latin alphabet sometimes has to insert an additional letter into a word to convey the true equivalent of a single Cyrillic character. Yet, despite these differences, the scholars' achievement was considerable; they had brought together the two largest South Slav linguistic groups, covering present-day Croatia, Serbia, Montenegro, and Bosnia-Herzegovina.

Without this task political union would have been impossible.

There are, however, two other languages extensively used in Yugoslavia. Slovene has affinities with Croatian, but is much further removed from it than Serbian is, despite the fact that both Slovene and Croatian use the Latin alphabet. Slovene is a comparatively old tongue; its earliest books were printed four hundred years ago. Today it is recognized as the official language of the north-western republic. The Macedonian language, which has a similar status down in the south, is very different; it is nearer to Bulgarian than to Serbo-Croat and has achieved a literary form only in the last two decades. The first Macedonian grammar was published as recently as 1952 and the first scholarly dictionary did not appear until the end of 1961. Quite apart from the Slovene and Macedonian regions, there still remain towns and villages around the frontier where it is customary to speak Hungarian or Albanian or Roumanian or a dialect of Italian; there are, in fact, some 1,400 schools which use one or other of these 'minority languages' for their main lessons. Although Yugoslavia lacks linguistic uniformity, most of the people throughout the country understand Serbo-Croat and many have learnt one of the major European languages as well.

It is all too easy to make a false inference from this linguistic confusion. The South Slavs possess a rich literary heritage, even though the accepted written forms are of recent growth. Marin Drzić of Dubrovnik wrote lively comedies which have some of the spirit, if not the grace, of his contemporary, Shakespeare; they are still performed at the annual festival in Dubrovnik. A few years later Dubrovnik produced a great poetic dramatist, Ivan Gundulić. One of the scholars who 'created' the

Serbian language, Dositej Obradović, published a fascinating prose autobiography in the seventeen-eighties; there is an English translation. Fifty years later there was a remarkable group of lyric poets writing in their native language in Slovenia. And, in recent years, the Yugoslavs may claim an epic novelist of the first order in Ivo Andrić, a retired diplomat, who has found his literary inspiration in the tragic history of his native Bosnia, and who was awarded the Nobel Prize for Literature in 1961.

The real treasure pieces of Yugoslav culture are, how-ever, the popular ballads of the Serbs and Montenegrins (of which there are several good English translations). These stark records of warfare and struggle, with their rhythmic incantations of mighty heroes meeting saintly deaths, played a great part in creating a sense of patriot-ism before ever they were committed to paper, It was, moreover, their influence that led Petar Petrović Njegoš, the Prince-Bishop of Montenegro in the eighteen-thirties and eighteen-forties, to write the masterpiece of all Serbian literature, *The Mountain Wreath,* an imagina-tive poetic chronicle of Montenegro's history. Modern Yugoslavia has swept away the last vestiges of the clan-nish society which Njegoš dominated little more than a century ago, but even today his tomb high up on the Black Mountain itself is held in veneration by the Montenegrins.

Folk-ballads are, of course, the product of a peasant people with legends of their own to perpetuate, and we must not forget the close links between the Yugoslavs and the soil. Yugoslavia is still essentially a land of villages and market-towns. The 1953 census showed that fourteen of the seventeen million people in the country lived in small communities. Many of them were engaged in local industries, but over ten million (68 per cent.) were directly dependent on agriculture for their livelihood. The 1961 Census showed that the total population had increased by a million and a half and that there had been a drift away from the countryside and into the towns, but, even so, three out of five Yugoslavs still work on the land. Thirty years ago the proportion of the town population was very much smaller; and it is estimated to have been less than 18 per cent. in 1941. If there were reliable statistics for earlier periods, it would have been smaller still.

There is a tragic recurrent theme in the social history of all the Yugoslav regions except Slovenia; the struggle of far too many people to scrape a bare existence from far too little cultivable soil. Fertile plains comprise no more than an eighth of the land surface. To the north and west and south of them stretch range upon range of wild mountains. On some slopes forests provide valuable timber deposits, but elsewhere they form a limestone rampart with only small pockets of shrub and coarse grass. The economic implications of this situation will be examined in more detail in Chapter Three. For the moment it is enough for us to remember that the stubbly-chinned and toothless peasant, with his round black cap and saddle of blankets tied with cord, vainly encouraging a self-willed donkey to mount a rock-strewn path, is just as much a Yugoslav as the grey-suited official who sits swallowing plum brandies with Turkish coffee on the terrace of a small-town café. Perhaps the black caps and blanket saddles are on the way out, but for the moment they are there still, a reminder of the thousands who remain dependent for a good or bad year on the caprice of nature. Communism is only slowly making an impact on this way of life.

The predominance of agriculture in its more organized form has, however, had far-reaching social consequences. Even before the communists came to power, there were no 'ancient families' in the country. Under the old empires, most Yugoslavs had tilled the soil for Austrian or Hungarian or Turkish landowners. The fortunate ones had possessed small freeholdings, often in the less fertile regions. Industry barely existed before 1914, apart from a few factories in Slovenia, Croatia, and Voivodina. Indeed, in Serbia the peasants were so suspicious of the advance of industry that they could not be tempted away from the fields. When unskilled labour was required to lay railway-sleepers on the main trunk-route in the eighteen-eighties, the navvies had to be brought across from Italy; this, it seemed, was no work for a Serb. An ambitious young peasant would dream of leaving the land and becoming a petty official or, better still, an army officer. Many did—and returned to exercise an intolerable superiority over the class from which they had sprung. But all carried into the towns the stamp of the peasantry: a sturdy independence, a stubbornness that bordered on truculence, and a rare unpredictability in bargaining. Sometimes they showed a canniness that was mean; at other times a trust that was foolhardy. Many a Yugoslav family has a cautionary tale of the grandfather who went to town, back in the bad old days, and fell into the clutches of the money-lenders, with their impossible rates of interest.

In most parts of Yugoslavia peasant habits have permeated every section of society. In the early evening it is still possible to see in the towns an interesting survival of a village custom, common to most Mediterranean lands. Everyone who has nothing more pressing to do joins in the 'Corso', a sauntering promenade along a recognized section of the main street to meet friends and exchange the day's gossip. And nowadays, particularly on Sunday afternoons in Croatia, the townspeople strive rather self-consciously to preserve the traditional folk-music and dances of the villages from which their families came.

Both between the wars and since the formation of the Federation the ruling class in Yugoslavia has consisted of men of peasant stock. It is curious to reflect that ex-King Peter II is on his mother's side a great-great-grandson of Queen Victoria, while through his father he is a great-great-grandson of 'Black George', a rebellious Serbian pig-dealer of proven patriotic courage but distinctly disagreeable temper. President Tito, too, comes from the peasantry; his father was a Croatian farmer who, since he had fifteen children, had to eke out the uncertain profits from his small plot of land by acting as a carter on the estates of the Hungarian nobility who, at that time, dominated Croatia. Other leading Yugoslavs come from a similar environment.

This peasant background has posed a difficult problem in recent years, one that has not yet been fully solved. Since 1947 the Yugoslavs have mobilized their economic resources so effectively that industrial production quadrupled in thirteen years. But many of the workers who made possible this achievement were ex-peasants, who had gone into the factories because there was not enough work for them on the land. They showed remarkable enthusiasm, but they lacked experience and often made serious errors. There was no large class of skilled workers on which the communist administrators could draw. Moreover, the Yugoslav communist system has asked for even more than technical ability from its workers. In 1950 the Yugoslavs introduced workers' self-government into all state-owned economic enterprises. This interesting and ambitious experiment will be considered in more detail in Chapter Three. In the present context we must note that self-government in industry threw a considerable burden of business responsibility on the shoulders of largely untrained workers. The authorities within the local republics are seeking to combat this technical and administrative ignorance by a major system of adult education. It is difficult to assess its effects, but it is significant that whereas, when the 1953 Census was taken, one in four of the population was found to be unable to read or write, the figure had fallen to one in five by 1961 (and only one in fifty in Slovenia). There is, of course, a big difference between elementary literacy and skilled workmanship but, at all events, there seems to be a general rise in the standard of education.

There has been a shortage not only of skilled workers, but of managers as well. Many industrial undertakings between the wars depended on foreign capital to such a large extent that they were, in reality, owned by non-Yugoslav companies. French capital controlled copper-mines, hydro-electric works, coal-mines, and various heavy industries (including, incidentally, the factories of Jesenice, mentioned at the start of this chapter). Many other countries had interests: the British, for example, in lead and silver mines; and the Germans in textiles. These investments not only influenced the foreign policy of inter-war Yugoslavia; they also meant that it was rare for the managerial class to be South Slav, for foreign companies tended to give administrative positions to their own nationals. Even when the business-men were Yugoslav citizens, they were generally Jewish and, of course, the Jewish community suffered during the war years as grievously in Yugoslavia as in any other territory occupied by the Germans or their puppet régimes. All this meant that when the communists nationalized foreign-owned industries after the war, they found themselves short of skilled personnel at all levels. It has been only in the last six years that there have been clear signs of steady industrial growth. The material well-being of the Yugoslav town-dwellers at last appears to be improving, even to the outside observer.

In the north and west of the country we must include mass tourism as a major post-war source of national revenue. Yugoslavia is more accessible to the casual traveller from western Europe than any other communist state, and in recent years over six hundred thousand tourists have visited the country each summer, mainly Germans, Italians, Austrians, and British. Every visitor takes back, of course, his own impression. Some have returned home with criticisms—drab goods in shops not intended for the tourist, bad roads once one leaves the two main 'motorways', eccentric hotel plumbing, etc. Others have been relieved that there is not more external evidence of single-party dictatorship. ('We didn't see a single secret policeman!'). Discerning observers have commented on the extensive building projects, which are throwing up blocks of apartments, architecturally rather monotonous, in nearly every town. Yet others have noticed the high level of recent cultural achievements, on the stage (opera, ballet, drama) as well as in the visual arts and especially sculpture. (There was a successful exhibition of modern Yugoslav Art in London's Tate Gallery in the summer of 1961.) Some visitors have been surprised by the number of Yugoslavs who attend church on Sundays and festivals, especially in Croatia and Slovenia, for religious education is forbidden in the schools, as it is in all communist states. Yet the most abiding impression for the majority of visitors is of natural beauty, the grandeur of the mountains, and the delights of the Dalmatian coast with its fascinating chain of islands.

Many people who come to Yugoslavia for the first time are surprised by its extent. There is still a tendency to think of it as 'one of those little countries in the Balkans', a habit of thought that probably survives from some recollection of pre-1914 Serbia. Nowadays this description is inaccurate in two respects: the Balkan ranges proper extend into only a small segment of Serbia and Macedonia, the rest of the mountains of Yugoslavia being an extension of the Alps; and, in area, Yugoslavia is ninth among the thirty-six states of present-day Europe. It is indeed only half the size of France and two-thirds the size of Italy, but it is larger than the United Kingdom and covers three times the area of the Austrian Republic, that last remaining rump of the Empire which dominated most of the Yugoslav lands only half a century ago.

There remains one other basic feature of political geography which merits comment and is often overlooked. Yugoslavia shares an eighteen hundred mile land frontier with seven different countries—Italy, Austria, Hungary, Roumania, Bulgaria, Greece, and Albania. Thus Yugoslavia has more European neighbours than any other existing state, even the U.S.S.R. Even in a stable Europe such an exposed position would require an adroit foreign policy. Present divisions in Europe make the task even harder. These seven neighbours fall, at the moment, into four different categories in international affairs: two of them, Italy and Greece, belong to the North Atlantic Treaty Organization; three, who between them control a thousand mile stretch of the frontier (Hungary, Roumania, and Bulgaria), belong to the Russian-sponsored Warsaw Pact; while of the remainder, Austria is pledged to permanent neutrality and Albania, although expelled from the Warsaw Pact in 1961, remains opposed to the Yugoslav type of communism. It is largely because of this international position that Yugoslavia has become the European leader of the group of 'uncommitted nations'. Foreign policy rarely shows rigid consistency, but where it does follow a set course it is more often dictated by geographical necessity than by political principles. Hence it seems unlikely that Yugoslavia will change her present delicately-poised neutrality, unless there is a major re-adjustment of the international balance of power or a crisis of decomposition within Yugoslavia itself. These are matters that we may leave for later chapters of the book.

Among the nations of the 'Modern World' Yugoslavia can never aspire to the status of a Great Power. But that does not mean that its way of life is unworthy of study. Yugoslavia remains a fascinating land. It is the home of five peoples, moulded by four cultures, conditioned by three religions, and expressing themselves in two alphabets. Its history is as full of grandeur and tragedy as the old Serbian ballads. It is not a man-made paradise; for there is much that seems repugnant to those of us accustomed to a different tradition. It is a land of experiment—more firmly welded together today than ever before. It is also, and this is not always appreciated in Britain, a land of example for even younger nations in other continents who stand to gain from its errors no less than from its achievements. The Yugoslav Federation is a phenomenon which merits our attention, both for itself and for what it symbolizes.

# 2

## THE PAST

THE ABSENCE OF a unified South Slav state before the present century makes the past of Yugoslavia a more complicated subject of study than the past of Britain or of France. A detailed narrative history would examine not only the development of the various nationalities, but the fate of the great empires whose armies marched and counter-marched across the Yugoslav plains or used the mountains as a natural wall of defence. Such treatment is, unfortunately, beyond the scope of this book. We shall consider the distant past only in outline and shall concentrate on the last century and a half, on the creation of the 'First Yugoslavia', and on the development of the idea of a Yugoslav Federation.

Although the histories of Britain and Yugoslavia are so different in character, there was a period of some four hundred years when both lands formed a part of the same political unit, the Roman Empire. Belgrade, like London, is the site of a Roman fortress; and Pula, like St. Albans, has a Roman amphitheatre, although in a much better state of preservation. Yet, apart from classical remains, the Romans left only one permanent feature—a dividing line separating the Western Empire, controlled from Rome, from the Eastern (Byzantine) Empire, controlled from Constantinople. This division, which dates from A.D. 395, still distinguishes the area that uses the Latin alphabet from the area that uses the Cyrillic.

The Yugoslavs themselves were, of course, never subjects of the Roman Empire. While the Dalmatian-born Emperor Diocletian was building his palace at Split, the ancestors of the families who inhabit that palace today were living a nomadic existence in what is now the Ukraine. About the year 450 these Slavs slowly began to migrate westwards, probably because of a sudden increase in population. Between 586 and 626 one large group of Slavs, turning southwards, came down on Macedonia, fanned out north-westwards along the rivers, and even crossed the mountains into the present-day Austrian province of Carinthia. These wandering groups did not have any political organization and they were partially absorbed into the empires that surrounded them. Those who settled in Serbia, Croatia, Montenegro, and Macedonia came nominally under the overlordship of the Byzantine Emperors, although the Slavs further north were conquered by the Franks and formed part of Charlemagne's Empire (800-814).

While the Slovenes remained bound to the successive rulers of Austria for over a thousand years, the Croats had greater independence. For a time they even had rulers of their own; one of these, Tomislav, was crowned King of Croatia by the Pope in 924. The Papacy continued to support Croatian rulers until the end of the eleventh century, but in 1102 the Croat crown passed into the hands of Prince Koloman, who was also heir to the Hungarian throne. From 1102 to 1918 the ruler of Hungary was thus legally the ruler of Croatia as well. Koloman's territory did not, however, include the whole of present-day Croatia; some of the Dalmatian coastal towns were subject to the Byzantine Empire, while others were controlled by Venice. In 1254 the Hungarians extended their dominion from Croatia to include Bosnia. For this action the Hungarians had the backing of the Papacy, as the Bosnians had developed religious beliefs of their own (generally, but incorrectly, known as 'Bogomilism') and these were strongly opposed to Catholic practice. The Bosnians remained under the Hungarians until the end of the fourteenth century when, for a brief period, they had rulers of their own until the Turkish conquest of 1463.

The Serbs had settled in two areas: one of these was called 'Zeta', with boundaries that corresponded to the later Montenegro; the other was known as 'Rashka', and consisted of the River Morava and the land to the north-west of it. The development of Zeta and Rashka was delayed by wars with the Byzantine Emperors and with the Bulgars, who invaded and ravaged Rashka on several occasions. The two states were united for the first time in 1186 under the leadership of the warrior-chief, Stephen Nemanya. It was Stephen who formally adopted the Orthodox religion for his people; his descendants ruled as kings of Serbia from 1196 to 1371. The greatest of these Nemanyid kings, as they are called, was Stephen Dušan, who was born in 1309 and reigned from 1331 until his death in 1355. Dušan's lands included not only Serbia and Montenegro, but Albania, Macedonia (except for Salonika), and half of present-day Greece as well; indeed on Easter Day in 1346 he was crowned 'Tsar of the Serbs and Greeks' at a solemn ceremony in his capital, Skopje. It was as a warrior that Dušan made an impact on his world, but we today are more interested in his attempt to organize an empire and, above all, in the *Zakonik*, his code of laws, from which the historian may learn almost as much about mediaeval Serbia as he does about Norman England from Domesday Book.

Dušan's Serbia, with its not unfamiliar pattern of a powerful Church and a feudal baronage, did not long survive its 'Tsar'. A new warrior people, inspired by the fanatical Muslim religion, crossed over from Asia; these were the Turks. They settled in Europe for the first time (on the Gallipoli peninsula) a few months before Dušan's death. Within thirty years they had conquered Bulgaria and Macedonia and entered southern Serbia. There, on the plain of Kosovo, the Serbs fought and lost the most fateful battle in their history. On that bloody day in 1389—June 28th by our reckoning—the Serbian feudal nobility perished almost to a man. There followed five centuries of Turkish domination for Serbia and for her neighbours.

While western Europe was experiencing the conflicts of the Reformation and the rise of nation states, the majority of Yugoslavs found themselves sinking back into the status of dependent peasants, subject to Austrian or Hungarian or Turkish overlords. In Bosnia some of the old nobility saved their lives and their estates by adopting the Muslim religion when the Turks conquered the region, and they continued to own considerable tracts of land until after the First World War. Of course, some districts benefited from the centuries of foreign rule: thus, most of the ports along the Adriatic were controlled by Venice, and flourished so long as the Venetian Republic remained the main trading centre in the Eastern Mediterranean. But, in general, the Yugoslavs were 'a subject-people'. Two areas alone retained some independence: in Dubrovnik (then called Ragusa) merchants built up a rich trading community rivalling Venice and able to maintain itself by skilful diplomacy until the Napoleonic Wars; and the fierce Montenegrins cherished their undying feud with the Turks, withdrawing into the impenetrable fastness of the Black Mountain when expeditions came against them, only to emerge and start life again once the invaders had withdrawn.

Turkish rule in Serbia and Bosnia was not unbearably harsh. There were, of course, heavy taxes and, until 1638, a forced levy of boys to serve as slaves in the Sultan's bodyguard; but the Serbian Orthodox Church was allowed to flourish, and some Serbs even held minor administrative posts under the Turks. Yet a sense of Serbian nationalism lingered on. The people were reminded of the glories of mediaeval Serbia not only by the Church leaders, but by the ballad-mongers with their songs of 'A land that shall be purged of the stranger and a king who shall reign yet once more from Dušan's throne'. By the end of the eighteenth century this dream seemed near realization. Turkish power was declining, and government had become inefficient (and more tyrannical). Austrians and Turks had fought each other for decades across the Danube and its plains, and many Serbs had slipped into exile, joining Austrian regiments and thereby acquiring military experience. It was one of these peasant-soldiers who led the Serbian national revolt in 1804. In the Austrian Army he had been Sergeant Petrović, twice decorated for bravery; but the Serbs, with a mixture of fear and admiration, called him 'Karadjordje' ('Black George'). It was as members of the House of Karadjordjević that his descendants ruled Serbia and the First Yugoslavia.

Karadjordje sustained the Serbian Revolt for nine years. He defeated the Turks three times in pitched battles, he set up a state council in Belgrade, he authorized the foundation of Serbia's first high-school. But his violent moods made him many enemies among the Serbs themselves, and when, in 1813, the Turks re-captured Belgrade, his administration fell apart and he was forced to flee into the Austrian lands. Two years later one of the Serbs whom he had offended picked up the threads of resistance and began a second revolt against the Turks. This new leader was Miloš Obrenović. He may have lacked the strategic brilliance of Karadjordje, but he had ten times his cunning. When Karadjordje was rash enough to return, Miloš had him killed and sent his severed head to the Sultan of Turkey as a gesture of reconciliation. In 1817 the Sultan recognized Miloš as 'Prince of Serbia' and allowed the Serbs considerable powers of self-government. Although Turkish troops did not finally leave Belgrade until 1867, the two revolts at last reversed the decision of Kosovo. Nevertheless, the Serbian Principality covered only a quarter the area of the present Serbian Peoples' Republic; the Turks remained firmly in control of Bosnia, Macedonia, and the very heart of the old mediaeval kingdom, including Kosovo itself.

Meanwhile, conditions were changing in Croatia and along the Dalmatian coast. Since 1527 the Croats had, like the Slovenes, been subjects of the Habsburg Emperor in Vienna; so, too, had most of the Hungarians and many of the Serbs who had fled from the Turks. Croatia had never entirely disappeared as a political unit: it was allowed to have a regional assembly (Diet) of its own and a Governor appointed by the Emperor. Moreover, the Habsburg rulers had organized a special defensive zone (the 'Military Frontier') around the borders of Bosnia and Turkish-occupied Serbia. The Croats were good soldiers and some of them had been

---

1. (a) *Belgrade.* The view from the old Turkish fortress of the Kalemegdan, at the junction of the rivers Sava (left) and Danube, towards new Belgrade in the background.
   (b) *Mostar.* The main town of Herzegovina. In the centre the fifteenth-century Turkish bridge, several mosques, and in the background the Dinaric Alps.

1a

rewarded by the Habsburgs with land (especially in the Military Frontier) and titles of nobility; their descendants served in high office until the fall of the Habsburg Empire in 1918 and never accepted the Yugoslav State. But other Croats and Slovenes were excited by the new ideas that began to spread through Europe in the eighteenth century. The French Revolution as such meant little to them; but in 1809 Napoleon defeated the Austrian Habsburg Emperor, and incorporated the whole of Dalmatia (including Dubrovnik) and large sections of Croatia and Slovenia into the French Empire as the 'Illyrian Provinces'.

For four years the Illyrian Provinces were administered by a Napoleonic Marshal, Marmont, and received all the advantages of Napoleon's reformed government. Of course they had the burdens of French occupation as well, but these were no greater than the Austrians had imposed. The Croat soldiers merely exchanged service to one Emperor for another. Thus we find a Croat Regiment at the head of Napoleon's 'Grand Army' when it entered Moscow in 1812 (as a Yugoslav Colonel proudly recalled, in an address in London, during a recent moment of tension with the Russians). The interlude of French administration was brief, but it gave to the people of the Illyrian Provinces a sense of unity that lived on after the fall of Napoleon and the restoration of Austrian rule.

The dominant statesman of the Austrian Empire in the first half of the nineteenth century was Prince Metternich. He believed that the Empire (and Europe) needed a period of calm after the convulsions of the

2. (a) *Dubrovnik*. The fortifications of this ancient seaport and former independent republic.
   (b) *The Mountains of the Boka Kotorska*, Montenegro.

Napoleonic Wars. He was convinced that, in general, political nationalism was a danger to peace and stability, but he was prepared to encourage 'Illyrianism' among the Croats because he thought that it would counteract the more violent patriotism of the Hungarians. When Metternich fell in 1848 and the Empire was almost destroyed by a series of nationalist and liberal revolutions, the Croats remained loyal and took a prominent part in suppressing both the Hungarians and the Italians. But in 1867 the Emperor Francis Joseph reversed the earlier policy. Instead of restraining the Hungarians (in size, second only to the German-Austrians among the eleven nationalities in his Empire), he took them into partnership, creating what was known as the 'Dual Monarchy' of Austria-Hungary. The Croats were left in the Hungarian half of the Monarchy, while Dalmatia and the Slovene-speaking parts of the Illyrian Provinces were in the Austrian half. In 1868 the Hungarians agreed that the Croats should continue to have a Diet for local affairs and should send representatives to the Hungarian Parliament in Budapest, but there was little love lost between the two nationalities. With Illyrianism dead, some leading Croat intellectuals (including a prominent Roman Catholic Bishop, Joseph Strossmayer) began to think of a much broader South Slav movement to include the Serbs as well. By the end of the century more and more lawyers and teachers were turning their hopes to the Serbs; but the mass of the people remained too concerned with their everyday existence to be worried by such political considerations.

The Turkish Empire appeared to be breaking up more rapidly than the Austrian. As its central government decayed into inefficiency, so its local administrators became more brutal. In 1875 revolts flared up in Bosnia,

Herzegovina, and Bulgaria. They were put down with great cruelty. The Russians felt unable to stand by while the Turks were massacring their fellow-Slavs and co-religionists. In April 1877 Russia declared war on Turkey and was joined by Roumania, Montenegro, and Serbia. Nine months later the Russians made peace at San Stefano, on the outskirts of Constantinople. Serbia received complete independence and a small increase in territory, as also did Montenegro: but the Russians insisted on the creation of a Great Bulgaria, which they believed they would be able to control as a satellite state. This was unacceptable to the other European Powers and in the summer of 1878 a Congress at Berlin re-arranged the map of the Balkans. Serbia and Montenegro retained their gains, but Bulgaria was considerably reduced in size, and Austria-Hungary was given control of Bosnia and Herzegovina (although the two provinces remained technically Turkish). The Berlin settlement was to have important repercussions: the Serbs distrusted the new Bulgaria which, in fact, defeated them in a brief war in 1885; and the Bosnians resented being treated by the Austrians as if they were a conquered colonial people. When in 1908 the Austrians broke the last links with Turkey by annexing Bosnia-Herzegovina to the Dual Monarchy, this resentment became explosive—with disastrous consequences in 1914.

Serbia, meanwhile, was developing slowly. The Kingdom—as it became in 1882—had a parliamentary system and a written constitution; but there was a discrepancy between theory and practice. Once in parliament the politicians tended to become unscrupulous careerists who exploited the peasantry. Even the Crown was little more than a shuttlecock in the feud between the Obrenović and Karadjordjević families. For a time there seemed some prospect that Prince Nikita of Montenegro might become leader of the South Slavs; he modernized his state, which he declared a kingdom on the fiftieth anniversary of his accession (1910), but he was too grasping and petty to emerge as a statesman. Moreover, Montenegro was too isolated; it lacked Serbia's position on the Danube. Yet under the incompetent rule of King Milan Obrenović (1868-89) and his son, Alexander, the prestige of Serbia sank lower and lower until by the turn of the century it looked as if the state might pass under Austrian protection.

In June 1903 discontent with the feeble Obrenović rule led to a palace revolution in Belgrade, during which the King and Queen were butchered by young army officers. The rebels summoned to the throne Peter Karadjordjević, the grandson of 'Black George'. Peter had already distinguished himself as leader of a guerrilla band against the Turks in 1877, but he was more than a warrior. In his many years of exile, he had acquired a first-hand knowledge of liberal institutions. He saw to it that for ten years Serbia had genuine parliamentary government. Serbia prospered as never before. These achievements awakened the desire of the Serbs still under Turkish or Austrian rule to be united with the Serbian Kingdom. In the Balkan Wars of 1912-13 the Greeks, Serbs, Bulgars, and Montenegrins almost threw the Turks out of Europe. Serbia more than doubled its size: Kosovo was liberated, and so was Skopje; most of Macedonia was incorporated in the Serbian Kingdom and a common frontier was achieved with Montenegro. But success went to the Serbs' heads. There were still Serbs subject to the Emperor Francis Joseph. As Pašić, the Serbian prime minister, said; 'The first round is won; now we must prepare for the second, against Austria'.

The Serbian desire to liberate Bosnia became the immediate cause of the First World War. The ultimate origins of the war lie, of course, much further back, and especially in the emergence of two groups of alliances in Europe which were precariously balanced in suspicious rivalry. If Bosnia had not been the occasion of the war, then any one of half a dozen other places could have been. But, as it was, war came in 1914 as a direct result of the assassination of the heir to the Austrian throne by a Bosnian Serb, Gavrilo Princip, during a ceremonial visit to Sarajevo, tactlessly arranged for June 28th, Serbia's national day and the anniversary of Kosovo. The Serbian Government itself knew nothing of Princip's conspiracy. It may, however, have anticipated such an act, for ever since the Austrians annexed Bosnia in 1908 the youth of the province had been in a state of patriotic frenzy. From 1911 onwards they had received help from a secret terrorist organization with headquarters in Belgrade; this was officially called 'Unity or Death' but, because of its sinister activities, it was more generally known as the 'Black Hand'. Princip was a student of nineteen and some of the other conspirators were even younger (at least two of them are still alive, one being a distinguished historian). The group received arms from the leader of the Black Hand, Colonel Dimitriević, one of the 1903 palace assassins who was now chief of Serbian military intelligence. The Austrians were already irritated by years of Serbian hostility, and when they discovered that Princip's revolver came from the Serbian arsenal, they not unnaturally assumed the complicity of the Serbian Government. In fact, however, Dimitriević (whom the Austrians did not succeed in identifying as the author of the plot) was on bad terms with the government at the time and was executed in 1917 after a trial on trumped-up charges. But the Austrian Government was, anyhow, determined to destroy the Serbian hornet's nest. A harsh ultimatum was despatched from Vienna to Belgrade on July 23rd; five days later the Austrians declared war. The Serbs appealed for help to the Slav mother-nation, Russia; and, because of the system of alliances, most of Europe was at war within a week.

The Serbs fought with magnificent courage. After four months of war not a single Austro-Hungarian soldier remained on Serbian soil except as a prisoner, but the Serbs were not strong enough to carry a counter-offensive across the Danube. At the end of 1915 the Austrians, with German and Bulgarian support, launched another attack and overwhelmed the Serbs, who fell back through the mountains to Albania in the depth of winter. The survivors of this grim retreat, the horrors of which had been intensified by a typhus epidemic, were rescued from the Albanian coast and transported first to the Greek island of Corfu (where the Government remained) and subsequently to the Allied base at Salonika. The Serbs participated in the five-nation advance from Salonika in 1918, which carried them through the enemy fortifications and back into southern Serbia itself.

The Croats and Slovenes were, of course, conscripted into the Austro-Hungarian Army, but were generally used on the Russian and Italian Fronts rather than against Serbia. Some Croats escaped to serve the Allied cause and reached London and Paris. There they established a Yugoslav Committee to urge the Allied governments to encourage the union of Serbs, Croats, Slovenes, and Montenegrins after the war. The Committee did not have an easy task; British and French statesmen were lukewarm, although influential groups of intellectuals were well-disposed, and so, too, were the Americans; but the Italians, who wanted to acquire the Dalmatian coast, were openly hostile; and the Serbian Government itself distrustful. Pašić, the Serbian premier, was in his seventies and too set to welcome new ideas; he was a narrowly patriotic member of the Serbian Orthodox Church, and suspicious of Croats on both political and religious grounds. He wanted a 'Greater Serbia', which was to include much of Croatia and Dalmatia but over which the Serbs would be the master race. But in the summer of 1917 the president of the Yugoslav Committee, Ante Trumbić, went to Corfu. The war was going badly for the Allies at that time, and he was able to secure a solemn declaration from Pašić providing for the creation of a Kingdom of Serbs, Croats, and Slovenes in which all three peoples would receive equality before the law. This 'Corfu Pact' is the foundation charter of the Yugoslav State, although Pašić later insisted that it was not binding as Trumbić had no legal status. It is one of the tragedies of South Slav history that the rivalry between 'Greater Serbia' and 'Yugoslavia' continued for a quarter of a century after the signature of the Pact.

The Yugoslav Kingdom established after the First World War was not quite so extensive as the present Federation, but it was more than five times the size of Serbia at Peter's accession in 1903. Most of the South Slavs living under the old Dual Monarchy were united with those who, in 1914, had been living within the Serbian and Montenegrin Kingdoms. Serbia (as enlarged by the Balkan Wars) was joined to Croatia, almost the whole of Dalmatia, Bosnia-Herzegovina, much of the southern Hungarian Plain, and most of the Slovene-speaking parts of Austria. In addition, a small region was acquired from Bulgaria along the Macedonian frontier. Montenegro, too, joined the new state. Throughout the war Montenegro had been a separate kingdom allied to Serbia, but the Serbs succeeded in convincing their western European sympathizers that King Nikita had betrayed them to the Austrians in the retreat of 1915, and when, in 1918, a (hardly representative) Montenegrin Assembly voted for union with Serbia, the Great Powers accepted its verdict, and Montenegro lost its independence. Nikita's behaviour had, indeed, been characteristically tortuous—for how else could he have remained on his throne since 1860?—but there were many Montenegrins who resented the Serbian action and who continued a guerrilla campaign against the new administration for several years.

The Yugoslavs had claimed even more territory than they received. They had wanted northern Albania, another mountain-pass in Bulgaria, and a larger share of the Hungarian Plain. But the Paris Peace Conference refused to sanction these acquisitions, since it sought to base the new frontiers, as much as possible, on the idea of 'national self-determination'. For the same reason it prevented an attempt by the Yugoslavs to gain the Slovene-speaking district within Carinthia, the Austrian province beyond the Karawanken Mountains. The most serious dispute in which the Yugoslavs were concerned was over the frontier with Italy. In 1915 the Italians had secretly been promised considerable gains in return for entering the war on the Allied side, but much of the territory that they sought was inhabited by South Slavs, and the Italians did not get all that they wanted from the Peace Conference. From 1919 to 1923 there was tension between Italy and Yugoslavia. In the end the Italians retained control of three important regions where there were Yugoslav majorities: the port of Rijeka, which was then known by its Italian name of Fiume; the old Dalmatian city and harbour of Zadar (Zara in Italian); and the Istrian Peninsula. The Yugoslavs never abandoned hope of obtaining these areas and they were, indeed, ceded to the Federation after the Second World War.

The 'Kingdom of the Serbs, Croats, and Slovenes' was formally proclaimed on December 1st, 1918. Although there had been a movement in favour of unification for some eighty years, few of its inhabitants yet thought of themselves as Yugoslavs. In their own eyes they were, as they had always been, Serbs or Croats or Slovenes or Montenegrins. They passively accepted the new state, but it meant little to them. For some it even meant hardship—a frontier that in places separated a village from its traditional pastures, cut off old markets or, as at Fiume, divided a suburb from the town which had been its origin. From the first there were some groups who refused to accept the Yugoslav idea. Potentially the most dangerous of these were the half-million Germans who lived within the new frontiers; but there was great resentment, too, among the half-million people who regarded themselves as Hungarian and who were encouraged to continue their Hungarian loyalty by constant propaganda from Budapest. Later, as living conditions in the north became worse rather than better, the Croats and Slovenes joined the critics of the state.

King Peter of Serbia became the first sovereign of the unified kingdom but, as he was a sick man in his late seventies, his thirty-year-old son Alexander acted as Regent, succeeding to the throne in 1921. Two men determined the character of the First Yugoslavia, King Alexander and the veteran politician Pašić. As we have seen. Pašić was a Serb through and through, and in these last years of his life—he died in 1926—never became at heart a Yugoslav. Alexander was a more complex personality: his wartime bravery had won him admiration in Britain and France and he was idolized by the peasant soldiery of Serbia, but he was a difficult man, more reserved than his father had been, aloof and tense. He had received his military education at the Russian Tsarist Court, and would probably have married one of the Tsar's daughters had she not been murdered by the Bolsheviks. His Russian experiences made him believe in firm government and gave him an intense personal hatred of communism; while the fact that he had spent six years of his life as a military commander led him to expect a soldierly obedience from his new subjects which few of them were prepared to render.

Alexander at first accepted the need for a parliamentary constitution, but his natural distaste for democratic government was intensified by the fractious behaviour of the Yugoslav politicians. A climax was reached in 1928, when a Montenegrin Deputy turned his revolver on the Opposition Front Bench, killing the Croat Peasant leader and two of his colleagues. In this crisis Alexander kept his head—but at the expense of democracy. He rejected a Croatian demand for 'home rule' and imposed a royal dictatorship on the country, appointing the commandant of the Royal Guard as nominal prime minister. At the same time he changed the official name of the Kingdom to Yugoslavia, and tried to offset the local loyalties of the various peoples by doing away with the old historic divisions (Serbia, Croatia, etc.) and replacing them by administrative units named after geographical features. Alexander certainly regarded himself as first and foremost a Yugoslav; but he ruled almost entirely through Serbs. Nine out of every ten army officers were from Serbia, and in the twenty-three years of the First Yugoslavia there was only one period of five months when a non-Serb (in this case, a Slovene) was prime minister. The Croats, Slovenes, and Montenegrins could rightly claim that all this was far removed from the equal status for all nationalities promised in the Corfu Pact. The Croats had possessed more self-government under Hungarian rule.

Two of Yugoslavia's neighbours, Italy and Hungary, were prepared to exploit Croatian discontent for their own ends. The Italian fascist dictator Mussolini encouraged Croat exiles to organize a fascist movement of their own, called the *Ustaše*, and the Hungarians gave them training facilities near the Yugoslav frontier. A third neighbour, Bulgaria, secretly supported a Macedonian terrorist organization, the I.M.R.O. In 1934 these two groups formed an unholy alliance against King Alexander. The King had always relied on the friendship of France and of France's allies in Europe, particularly Czechoslovakia and Roumania. To strengthen these links Alexander accepted an invitation to pay a state visit to Paris in November 1934. He never reached Paris. Within half an hour of landing at Marseilles he had been shot by an I.M.R.O. assassin in *Ustaše* pay. There was genuine sorrow in Yugoslavia, even in those areas which had resented Alexander's heavy hand. It was a sorrow mingled with apprehension, for to many the Marseilles assassination seemed like another Sarajevo—in reverse. Since the conspiracy had been hatched on Hungarian soil, it looked for a few weeks as if the Yugoslavs would be at war with Hungary. The League of

Nations succeeded in keeping peace between the two states and tension gradually eased; but the murder left Yugoslavia without a natural leader. The next strong man to emerge in the country was at that moment in hiding in Zagreb, after languishing for six years in Alexander's prisons; he was a communist engineer, shortly to take the code-name of Tito.

Alexander was succeeded by his son, Peter II, but as he was only eleven years of age the royal powers were entrusted to three Regents, of whom the most important was Alexander's cousin, Prince Paul. There was no change in the spirit of the administration, but the Serbian political leaders acquired more influence now that Alexander's masterful personality was gone. These were years in which the European balance changed decisively. The French and their allies declined in influence, and between 1936 and 1939 central and eastern Europe gradually came under the economic and political dominance of Germany and Italy, the so-called 'Axis Powers'. In March 1938 Hitler annexed Austria to Germany, and German troops appeared for the first time on Yugoslavia's frontiers. In April 1939 the Italians occupied Albania, giving the Axis yet another point from which to enter Yugoslavia. Inevitably the Yugoslav Government let its contacts with western Europe drop and sought to establish friendlier relations with Germany and Italy.

Ironically, it was at this moment of international crisis that a settlement was reached in the feud between the Croats and the Serbs. In August 1939 the Croatian areas were authorized to establish a local assembly (Diet) of their own, although Defence and Foreign Affairs were left in the hands of the Belgrade Government. At the same time the leading Croatian politician was made a

Vice-Premier. Although all Croats except the extremists were satisfied by this agreement, it was resented by the Slovenes and Macedonians (who were still governed directly from Belgrade) and detested by many of the more conservative Serbs.

Any gain that there might have been in internal security was, however, rapidly offset by the deteriorating situation abroad. In September 1939 the Germans invaded Poland, and the British and French, who were Poland's allies, declared war on Germany. But no allied help reached Poland, and the country (half as big again as Yugoslavia) was overrun within a month. The war continued, but across the long frontier between France and Germany there was little activity. For eight months the opposing armies eyed each other suspiciously from their fortified lines. And for eight months all Europe, including Yugoslavia, watched anxiously for the next move. Then on May 10th, 1940, the Germans launched a great offensive with their swift-moving tank divisions, not only against the British and French, but through neutral Holland and Belgium as well. The Dutch were defeated within four days; the Belgians within twenty days. And seven weeks from the opening of the on-slaught, German troops were in Paris and the French surrendered. Only the British, secure behind the natural tank-barrier of the Channel, continued to resist Hitler. Never before had the balance of power changed so swiftly in Europe.

These events influenced the political attitude of all the European nations, not least the Yugoslavs. For Yugoslavia had modelled her army and her air force on the French. Less than four years previously the French General Gamelin, whose armies had now been scythed down by the German tank-thrust, had advised the Yugo-slavs on the best way to defend themselves. Then it had been assumed that France and Yugoslavia and Italy would be fighting on the same side against Germany. Now the French were knocked out and the Italians, instead of fighting alongside the French, belatedly entered the Second World War on the German side. Small wonder that the timid Yugoslav Government felt dismayed.

The Yugoslavs remained inactive while German troops were permitted to move across two more neighbouring countries, Hungary and Roumania, officially to protect Roumania's oilfields from the British. When in October 1940 the Italians launched an attack on Greece from their Albanian bases, some members of the Yugoslav Government even wanted to enter the war on the Italian side (although nothing more was heard of this idea once the Greeks started to throw the Italians back). Prince Paul's personal sympathies were with Britain; he had been an undergraduate at Christ Church, Oxford, and he was married to the sister of Princess Marina of Kent. But he saw himself as the head of a country that was ill-armed and only loosely united. He dared not provoke a German attack, for, as he told the American Minister in Belgrade, he believed his army could not resist an invasion for more than a fortnight. There seemed to be none of the spirit of 1914-15.

Prince Paul's Government was becoming more and more unpopular. The younger generation had long struggled against its dictatorial tendencies, and the veter-ans of the 1912-18 wars hated the Germans and Italians. Discontent was encouraged by British agents. The climax was reached in March 1941, when the Germans required

Yugoslavia to sign an alliance with them in Vienna. Knowing the temper of the country, the Yugoslav Ministers slunk off to Vienna at night from a suburban railway-station. They arrived back in Belgrade on the morning of March 26th. At 2 a.m. in the following night Yugoslav air force officers seized the capital in a bloodless *coup d'état*. The Regency was abolished and Prince Paul forced to leave the country. King Peter II assumed his royal duties and a new government was formed under General Simović, who it was believed would be more friendly towards the British. There was great excitement throughout Belgrade and violent anti-German demonstrations. Some of the thousands in the streets were singing patriotic songs and waving tricolour flags; some had red flags and shouted communist slogans. But one cry above all others was caught up by the whole crowd: '*Bolje rat nego pakt—Bolje grob nego rob*' ('Better War than Pact—Better Grave than Slave'). The simple jingle, with its magnificent defiance and tragic foreboding, symbolizes the spirit of the day. Within a fortnight seventeen thousand of Belgrade's citizens were to lie dead among the ruins of the streets in which they had rejoiced; but March 27th, 1941, has remained a proud day for the Yugoslavs ever since.

The news of the events in Belgrade threw Hitler into a frenzy. Within ten hours of the *coup d'état* and without waiting to discover the policy of the Simović Government, Hitler gave orders for 'the destruction of Yugoslavia militarily and as a national unit'. Had Hitler been less hasty this action might not have been necessary; for the Simović Government was far more cautious than the people in the Belgrade streets. It refused to make joint war-plans with the British. It kept its inadequately armed troops thinly stretched out along fourteen hundred miles of frontier. It waited and hoped that the onslaught would not come; but in vain.

At dawn on April 6th, 1941, without a declaration of war, German dive-bombers fell on Belgrade. The city was undefended and hopelessly unprepared for the attack. Within forty-eight hours the centre of Belgrade was a heap of rubble; it was still smouldering when German troops entered a week later. Some units of the Yugoslav army resisted bravely, but two Croat regiments mutinied and operations were hampered by the German-speaking minority, who carried out acts of sabotage. On April 15th King Peter and the Government were evacuated by air from Montenegro. Two days later the Yugoslav army officially surrendered.

The Germans and Italians proceeded to divide up Yugoslavia. They annexed large sections of the country and gave other regions to their allies, Hungary and Bulgaria. In Zagreb the Italians set up an 'Independent State of Croatia' under the control of the *Ustaše* and its leader, Ante Pavelić. The Croatian State extended as far east as the approaches to Belgrade and included the whole of Bosnia-Herzegovina. Within these boundaries Pavelić established such a brutal tyranny that even the Nazi commander in Zagreb protested. An Italian Duke was proclaimed King of Croatia but, perhaps wisely, never visited his 'Kingdom'. The Italians also established a 'Kingdom of Montenegro' (the throne of which remained vacant), while the Germans set up a small Serbian State and induced a former War Minister to head a puppet government. Meanwhile, the legal Yugoslav Government continued a somewhat quarrelsome existence in exile, first in Cairo and later in London.

From the first some Yugoslavs had determined to resist the invaders and had kept their weapons. A group of regular soldiers, commanded by Colonel Draža Mihailović, withdrew into the mountains of south Serbia. In the course of September 1941 these 'Chetniks', as they were called, were in action against the Germans. The skirmishes were reported by radio to the exiled Yugoslav Government, who informed their allies that in Mihailović the Yugoslavs had found a patriotic resistance leader. In January 1942 he was promoted to General and given the official status of War Minister. The British supported him, sent liaison officers by parachute, and allowed his agents to use the B.B.C.'s external services for sending code messages. Mihailović, however, had his own ideas on the conduct of operations. Although personally a courageous man, he was short of weapons and wanted to wait for an allied invasion before ordering his men to attack the enemy. To avoid reprisals he would meanwhile hold his soldiers back. Politically, Mihailović believed in a 'Greater Serbia' just as Pašić had in the previous generation. He hated the Croats, whom he believed had stabbed the Serbian-dominated army in the back during the brief April campaign. But to his eyes there was an enemy greater than the Croats, and greater even than the invader; this was international communism, which in Yugoslavia was represented by the rival resistance movement, the Partisans. The Chetniks fought against the Partisans; and some Chetnik commanders collaborated with the German and Italian occupation forces. By the summer of 1943 Mihailović had become so involved in a civil war against the communists that Winston Churchill decided to withdraw British support from the Chetniks and give it to the Partisans.

Partisan resistance had been planned by the leaders of the Yugoslav Communist Party, meeting secretly in

Belgrade during May and June 1941, and the first operations against the Germans and the Italians took place in
mid-summer, some two months before the Chetniks
went into action. It is as well here to interrupt the
narrative of the war years and examine in some detail
the evolution of this Yugoslav communism and the
personality of its leader; for, although many of the men
and women who fought with the Partisans were not
communists, it was the Party which moulded out of the
resistance a force that was both patriotic and revolutionary.

The Communist Party had been formed in April 1919,
but there had been Marxists in the South Slav lands for
many years previously. The young men of Sarajevo, for
example, had evolved their own peculiar mixture of
socialist theory and patriotic sentiments before the most
notorious of them fired that fatal shot in 1914. Something of the spirit of these 'Young Bosnians' lived on in
the new Party. It won support rapidly. In the first
General Election (1920) it emerged as the third largest
party in the country, with more than a quarter of the
parliamentary seats; and it won municipal majorities in
a number of towns, including Zagreb. The Government
became alarmed, and in the following year had the
Party outlawed. Repression at first reduced numbers but
ultimately strengthened the movement by necessitating
strict discipline. Membership became an honour which
was bestowed only on proven revolutionaries. By 1941
the Party had a nucleus of twelve thousand members
and a youth organization of some thirty thousand. While
the youth movement was based on the University of
Belgrade, the secret Party headquarters were in Zagreb.
There were three reasons for the choice of this city: it
was an industrial centre; its citizens were already dis-

contented by years of Serbian predominance; and it was the home of the General Secretary, an engineer called Josip Broz, who had taken the conspiratorial name of Tito.

We have already, in the last chapter, noticed Tito's peasant background. He had been born in May 1892 in the tiny village of Kumrovec in Croatia, some thirty miles north-west of Zagreb. Thus he was a member of the same generation as Hitler (born 1889) and King Alexander (born 1888); or, to use communist comparisons, he was thirteen years younger than Stalin but two years older than Khrushchev. As a sergeant in the Austro-Hungarian Army in the First World War, Tito was wounded and captured by the Russians. He thus witnessed the Russian Revolution of 1917 as a prisoner-of-war working on the Trans-Siberian Railway. He became an ardent Bolshevik and, returning to Kumrovec in 1920, enrolled in the local Communist Party. In 1928 he fell into a trap set by the police, was discovered to possess bombs and a revolver, and was imprisoned. He was released in 1934 and found his way to Moscow, where he spent twelve months being trained as a political organizer. He became General Secretary of the Party on his return and in 1937 set about making it efficient. Apart from brief visits to Moscow in 1938 and 1939, he remained in Yugoslavia until, as Marshal Tito, he was flown to liberated Italy in 1944 to meet Churchill. On March 27th, 1941, he was in Zagreb, but hurried to Belgrade to concert arrangements with the Serbian and Montenegrin party leaders. With his smart suits and air of authority, he was more like a business executive than a communist conspirator. Prison had, as he said, been a university for him; he had read widely, and became a good linguist and an expert chess-player, having made his chessmen out of pieces of bread. In those arid summer days of 1941, while the Germans and their allies were invading Russia on a 2,500-mile front, Tito held councils of war hidden in the suburban villa of a rich newspaper proprietor who was a secret communist. His visitors have noted that Tito seemed much younger than his forty-nine years. He was to need that vitality in the months ahead.

The Partisan War is without parallel in the military history of Europe. The nearest equivalent is the guerrilla campaign waged by the Spanish against Napoleon. Yet the Yugoslav experience was something greater; it was both war of resistance and social revolution. Moreover, it was a war that involved the whole population; women fought in the mountains alongside the men. There was no one centre of revolt. Partisan bands struck first in Serbia on July 7th, 1941. Six days later the revolt spread to Montenegro. On July 22nd it was the turn of Slovenia, and on July 27th of Croatia and of Bosnia. The Macedonians joined in on October 11th. The enemies, in the first instance, were the Germans and Italians, and for a few days in September 1941 Partisans and Chetniks fought side by side. But inevitably the conflict became a civil war as well as a struggle against the invader, and the Partisans found themselves fighting Germans, Italians, Hungarians, Bulgarians, Serbs in German pay, Chetniks, and *Ustaše*. Between November 1941 and June 1944 the Germans launched seven major offensives against the Partisans, but never succeeded in eliminating them. The scale of the fighting may be estimated from a gloomy despatch sent by the German commander-in-chief in December 1943, in which he reported his failure to destroy the Partisans, even though he had under his command in Yugoslavia 360,000 men, of whom 200,000 were members of the German army. He estimated that the Partisans numbered 111,000 (although the figure was actually nearer 150,000).

Tito and the Partisan High Command never stayed for more than a few weeks in any one place. They moved along the mountain-chain that runs from Croatia through Bosnia-Herzegovina and Montenegro to southern Serbia. By escaping 'into the woods' they constantly shifted the main fighting front. The enemy would move in on a town only to discover that the Partisans had cleared out the night before; and he would take vengeance on the inhabitants. It was a bitterly cruel war. In some places pitched battles would be fought for days at a time. It took the Partisans a week to force a crossing of the Naretva, that narrow but deep mountain stream along whose valley thousands of tourists now pass each summer on their way from Dubrovnik to Sarajevo. On several occasions the Germans came near to liquidating the High Command. In a surprise parachute attack on headquarters at Drvar on May 24th, 1944 the Germans even captured Tito's Marshal's uniform, which they proudly sent to Vienna for exhibition. But the owner of those elegant trousers, those shining boots, had slipped away yet again. And when, only four months later, the Russians turned the German flank in the Balkans and pushed along the Danube and into Yugoslavia itself, Tito's men had advanced to within twenty miles of Belgrade.

Twice during the Partisan War Tito held political congresses in liberated towns. Technically, these congresses were meetings of A.V.N.O.J. (Anti-Fascist National Liberation Committee of Yugoslavia), an unofficial parliament with delegates from all parts of the country, some of whom were members of non-communist political parties. The first meeting, at Bihać in November 1942, elected an Executive Committee which was headed by Ivo Ribar, the former Speaker of the Yugoslav Parliament, a member of the Serbian Democratic Party. The congress passed a resolution guaranteeing the Yugoslav peoples' 'true democratic rights' and 'the inviolability of private property' after the invaders had been cleared from the country. At the second A.V.N.O.J. congress, at Jajce on November 29th, 1943, more revolutionary decisions were taken. The National Liberation Committee assumed the powers of a provisional government and resolutions were carried demanding the establishment of a republican and federal administration in post-war Yugoslavia. At the same time, on a motion from the Slovene delegates, the congress formally bestowed on Tito the newly created title of 'Marshal of Yugoslavia'. Although two more years were to elapse before Yugoslavia became officially a republic, the Jajce resolutions showed clearly enough from which direction the political wind was blowing.

The Partisans had received help from the British throughout the fifth, sixth, and seventh German offensives. The first British officers were dropped by parachute near Partisan detachments in May 1943. A full-scale military mission, headed by Brigadier Fitzroy Maclean (a Conservative M.P.), followed four months later. As the allies advanced in Italy, it became possible for the Royal Navy to ferry supplies from the Italian port of Bari, and the R.A.F. flew many sorties to aid the Partisans. But the general strategy of the war dictated that it should be the Russian Red Army that entered Belgrade with the Partisans in October 1944. This was to be of considerable political significance, for it confirmed the communist character of the Partisan movement.

The first occasion upon which British Commonwealth troops encountered the Partisans produced tension. This was at the Italian port of Trieste in May 1945, which had been occupied by New Zealanders although the Partisans were in the suburbs. The Yugoslavs claimed the right to administer the port, as the area around Trieste was inhabited by Slovenes. The British maintained that the town itself was Italian and that they needed the harbour facilities to supply the armies occupying northern Italy and Austria. For seven weeks the British and the Partisans faced each other with guns at the ready, but eventually a compromise was reached leaving the British administering the port. This was only the start of the Trieste problem; for the Yugoslavs strongly opposed the return of the city to Italy as part of the new peace settlement. Agreement was not reached until 1954, when Trieste was confirmed as an Italian city, although most of the land which had been occupied by the Partisans was allowed to remain in Yugoslavia. But in 1945 this was far ahead. For the moment the Trieste crisis had the effect of weakening Tito's links with the West and strengthening his dependence upon the Russians.

Relations between Britain and Yugoslavia also deteriorated because of Tito's attitude to the Yugoslav monarchy. The exiled royalist Government had been consistently opposed to the Partisans and until the end of 1943 insisted on regarding Mihailović and his Chetniks as the only resistance movement in the country. The British put pressure on King Peter and his Ministers to reach agreement with Tito, and in June 1944 Dr. Šubašić, the prime minister of the exiled Government, signed a declaration with Tito providing for an administration that would unite Tito's 'National Liberation Movement' and the Royal Yugoslav Government. Mihailović was thereupon officially dismissed by the King (but refused British offers of evacuation and remained in hiding in Serbia). In March 1945 the King agreed to the formation of a government in which Tito would be prime minister, but in which four of the exiled politicians would hold office, Šubašić being Foreign Minister. Nothing was said about the return of the King.

Meanwhile, the Partisans had set up 'Committees of National Liberation' to control the areas occupied by their forces. These Committees were closely modelled on the Russian Soviets and it rapidly became clear that Tito still intended, at a convenient moment, to put into effect the Jajce Resolution abolishing the monarchy. With Russian backing Tito gradually edged out the royalist politicians. Only one of them was still in office in November, 1945, when elections were held for the new parliament. There were no opposition candidates in this election. The voters, as in Russia, declared themselves for or against a list of 'National Front' delegates. Those who opposed the list recorded their vote in a separate ballot box. People who had been guilty of 'active or passive collaboration with the enemy' were not allowed to vote. 90.5 per cent. of the voters duly declared their acceptance of the National Front. With this evidence of support behind him, Tito went ahead with his plans to abolish the monarchy. On November 29th, 1945— exactly two years after the Jajce Resolutions—the new parliament proclaimed Yugoslavia a republic. Ivo Ribar became the first President.

There is no doubt that the mass of the country supported Tito in 1945, even if the election hardly accorded with British ideas of a popular ballot. The Communists had brought into politics the millions who had been ignored by former governments and whom the tragedy of war had, for the first time, made conscious of their Yugoslav identity. The Constitution of January 1946 emphasized the new character of the country in two ways: it established the six federal units, 'the People's Republics' (which were examined in the last chapter); and it included a statement of the basic principles of a socialist economy. In 1947 a Five-Year Plan, again on the Soviet model, indicated how these principles were to be put into practice.

There remained two groups fundamentally opposed to the new Yugoslavia: those devoted to the 'Greater Serbia' idea, and the Roman Catholic Church. The first of these was swiftly liquidated. In March 1946 the police at last captured Mihailović. Three months later he was put on trial in Belgrade, charged with raising an army to check Partisan resistance and with war crimes. Twenty-three other enemies of communism were charged with him, some of whom had been notorious collaborators while others were political leaders who had been, and still were, in exile. The trial dragged on for five weeks, and in the course of it Mihailović aroused sympathy among some foreign observers by his courage and fortitude. The verdict was, perhaps, inevitable. Eleven defendants, including Mihailović, were sentenced to death. He was shot on July 17th, 1946. To many people, it seemed as if Mihailović in the course of his trial had spoken his own epitaph: 'I wanted much, I began much, but the gale of the world swept away me and my work.'

Roman Catholicism posed a different type of problem for the Government, for it was both an internal political question and part of the wider conflict between two international creeds, one spiritual and one material. In

1941 there had been five and a half million Roman Catholics in Yugoslavia, most of them in Slovenia, Croatia, and Dalmatia. During the war many Church leaders had supported the *Ustaše*, and even those who did not were opposed to 'atheistic communism'. Some churchmen fled the country in 1945, but the head of the Church in Croatia, Archbishop Aloysius Stepinac, remained and for fifteen years was a centre of controversy. As a young man Stepinac had supported the idea of a united South Slav state, but between the wars he had come to resent the way in which the Serbs dominated the Catholic Croats. When the First Yugoslavia disintegrated in 1941, Stepinac instructed his clergy to accept the 'Independent State of Croatia'. He himself appeared side by side with Pavelić and the other *Ustaše* leaders at official functions (as, of course, his duty as Metropolitan of Croatia demanded that he should). His supporters maintain that, at the same time, he was trying to control the intolerance of the Croat extremists, and was secretly helping the Jewish and Serbian victims of oppression. In 1945, recognizing that the Archbishop was a man of considerable character, Marshal Tito met him at Zagreb in the hope that it would prove possible to avoid a conflict between Church and State. But although the meeting was a cordial one, Stepinac continued to condemn publicly what he regarded as the infringement of Church rights in education and the confiscation of Church property by the new authorities. He was arrested in September 1946, charged with having 'collaborated' with the *Ustaše*, and sentenced to sixteen years imprisonment. After serving five years he was released, and allowed for the rest of his life to act as priest in his native village, but he was not permitted to carry out his archiepiscopal duties. When, in 1952, Pope

Pius XII created Stepinac a Cardinal, the Yugoslav Government informed him that he could travel to Rome for the ceremony of institution, provided that he did not attempt to return to Yugoslavia. This offer Stepinac firmly rejected; until his death in February 1960 he remained unreconciled to the Government, a symbol of passive resistance for his co-religionists. Relations between Church and State appear to have improved under the Archbishop's successor, Mgr. Seper (as we shall see in Chapter Four).

Yugoslavia, in the eyes of the Western Powers, was little more than a satellite state of Russia throughout 1946 and 1947. A Red Army Military Mission remained in the country, Soviet experts were at hand to advise on the Five-Year Plan, and when disputes arose between Tito and the Americans, the Soviet representative in the Security Council served as ventriloquist for the Yugoslav dummy. Yet in reality tension was mounting between Moscow and Belgrade. In the immediate post-war years local communists came to power throughout most of eastern Europe, but in only two of the newly communist states (Yugoslavia and Albania) were the rulers people who had remained in the country and resisted throughout the war. The other leaders, as Tito once cuttingly remarked, 'had liberated their country by flying in afterwards, smoking a pipe'. Tito, having waged war as he wished, was not prepared to surrender his freedom of decision in time of peace. Friction between Russia and Yugoslavia began over comparatively trivial matters—the behaviour of Russian officers, the recruitment of Yugoslav citizens as Soviet spies— but became more serious when Tito refused to accept a Russian-sponsored Director-General for a joint Soviet-Yugoslav Bank, which Stalin personally wished to set up. The climax came early in 1948. The Russians accused the Yugoslavs of pursuing an independent line in their relations with their Balkan neighbours. The Yugoslavs, for their part, rejected Stalin's demand that Yugoslavia and Bulgaria should immediately unify their political and economic systems and form an entirely new state (which would have been more dependent on Moscow).

No communist leader had ever successfully defied Stalin; and the Russians did not believe that they would have much difficulty in bringing the Yugoslavs to heel. From March to June of 1948 serious wrangles took place in secret between the rival leaders. In a series of letters Stalin labelled Tito with every damning phrase in the communist vocabulary. But instead of withering before this Russian invective, Tito patiently but firmly replied to the accusations. The pressure was increased; Russian economic experts and military advisers were withdrawn from Belgrade. But although two leading Serbian communists supported Stalin rather than Tito, the Russians failed to break the essential unity of the Yugoslav Party Committee. On June 28th (that recurrently ominous date in South Slav history) the World was informed, from a Soviet-controlled Czechoslovak newspaper, that by its failure to suppress capitalism and by its 'limitless ambition, arrogance, and conceit' . . . 'the Yugoslav Party has put itself outside the family of fraternal Communist Parties, outside the united Communist Front'. This was the verdict of an assembly of international communist leaders (the Cominform), meeting in Bucharest. Tito had been expelled. Stalin waited for the defiant Yugoslav Government to collapse. 'I will shake my little finger—and there will be no more Tito,' he said.

Yet when Stalin died in March 1953 Tito was still in power in Belgrade—or rather he was at that moment on an official visit to London. For the Yugoslavs, proud of their independence, had responded to Russian dictation in 1948 as the people of Belgrade had responded to German dictation in 1941 or Austrian in 1914. Tito's prestige was enhanced rather than diminished by the attacks made on him, and the country supported him. He had in the end the sweet satisfaction of victory. For on May 26th, 1955 Stalin's successor, Khrushchev, visited Belgrade and, referring to the events of 1948, publicly declared his regret at what had happened and his repudiation of Stalin's accusations. It was an act of reconciliation without precedent in the history of Russian communism, but if it was intended to heal the wounds of the previous seven years, it failed. The Yugoslavs would not enter the bear's embrace a second time— they had been clawed once already, and their economy was still smarting. Yugoslavia has sought to remain free from foreign commitments; even a temporary agreement made in 1953 with Greece and Turkey, to provide for joint defence of the Balkans, was allowed to lapse as soon as possible. The Yugoslavs hope, by keeping clear of the Power blocs, to gain the moral leadership of peoples who, like themselves, seek to realize their destiny without interference from other states.

The breach with Russia in 1948 may have meant hardship for the Yugoslavs, but it also gave them the freedom to experiment. As machinery and oil and fertilizers ceased to arrive from the Soviet-controlled countries, so the Five-Year Plan was substantially modified, and the Yugoslavs struck out on a new economic policy of their own. Changes were made in the Soviet-inspired constitution and in the system of management in industry and agriculture. But this evolution of a specifically Yugoslav type of Socialism belongs essentially to the present, not to the past. The Yugoslav Revolution is over; the experiment in living continues.

# 3

## FOUNDATIONS AND LIMITS

U NTIL RECENT YEARS the Yugoslav lands were, economically, among the most backward in Europe. Their development has, in part, been hampered by their turbulent history and by the political frontiers which used to cut across them. But barriers of geography have afforded an even greater obstacle to progress. The country rests, as it were, on a north-west to south-east axis. The distinctive geographical features tend to follow this direction in parallel divisions and, since roads and railways in a mountainous country lie along the river valleys, so too do the main routes of communication. Ever since the establishment of the Yugoslav State in 1918 it has been difficult to move directly from north to south or—and this has had greater economic significance—from east to west. Geography has thus prevented Yugoslavia from becoming a natural economic unit.

Geographers normally divide Yugoslavia into three regions: the northern lowlands, the eastern plateau, and the western highlands. This is, perhaps, an oversimplification; for there are really six natural geographical zones. The first of these is an extension of the Alps, which covers western Slovenia, and makes its formation similar to that of southern Austria. Then along the Adriatic Sea there is a narrow strip of coastal plain which has Mediterranean vegetation and a typical Mediterranean climate of hot, dry summers and warm, wet winters. Behind this plain and running southwards from the Ljubljana Gap comes the third zone, the Dinaric Chain of mountains, which is subdivided into a higher, inland range (not unlike the Alps in formation) and a lower, coastal range of limestone. The Dinaric Chain, which runs down the entire country, broadening in the south and overflowing into Albania and Greece, is cut by a number of short, fast-flowing streams, none of which is navigable, and by a deep fjord, the Boka Kotorska. It thus forms a most effective natural divide, transversing Yugoslavia with a range of peaks which are in places over 6,000 feet high. The mountains are, moreover, both a climatic barrier and a watershed. The lands to their east experience a 'continental' climate, with wide ranges in temperature from January to July and with rainfall that is highest in May and June; and most of this area drains into the Danube or its tributaries, and thus eventually into the Black Sea. The fourth and fifth of our six zones lie in this region, to the east of the Dinaric Chain. The larger zone comprises the alluvial plains of the rivers Danube and Sava, stretching from Maribor (on the Austrian frontier) in a belt along the border of Hungary and into the Voivodina. This rich granary of wheat and maize and oats is essentially an extension of the Hungarian Plain. The smaller zone is a corridor between the Balkan and the Dinaric Chains; it stretches south-eastwards from Belgrade along the valleys of the Morava (a tributary of the Danube) and the upper Vardar (which flows southwards into the Aegean). This

3. *Agricultural Activities.*
   (a) Mountain pasture in Slovenia.
   (b) Drying tobacco on a wall in Macedonia.

4. *Old and New in Industry.*
   (a) Sawmills driven by mountain streams in Bosnia.
   (b) The generators at the Jablanica (Herzegovina) hydro-electric plant.

3a

5b

5a

6

region, too, contains good agricultural country and forests, but it is on a higher level than the Danube Basin, much of it forming a plateau over 1,000 feet above sea-level. Finally, the sixth region comprises the Balkan Mountains proper, which sweep across Macedonia in yet another barrier, intersected only by the River Vardar. Although the highest mountain in Yugoslavia (Triglav, 9,400 feet) is in northern Slovenia on the Austrian frontier, the Macedonian ranges have five peaks over 8,000 feet high. Over the centuries the Vardar Valley has, in consequence, been a valuable route of communication.

For, in a country of this character, the natural means of contact has been along the great rivers. The Yugo-slavs have always made good use of the Danube, and before the war sent most of their exports down the river and into the Black Sea for shipment to the wider world through the Bosphorus, or up the river to Central Europe. Goods from Zagreb were likewise carried down the Sava and thus into the Danube, and from Maribor down the Drava, another tributary. The political condi-tions of the inter-war years, when Serbia dominated the rest of the Kingdom, also contributed to the neglect of the Adriatic ports. Many Serbian exporters preferred to send their products, if not along the Danube, then down the Morava-Vardar valleys to Salonika, where the Greeks allowed the Yugoslavs special rights. This inter-war system of communications was, to some extent, a reflec-tion of even earlier conditions. When the country was first united in 1918, railways linking the various pro-

5. (a) *Split*. Statue of Bishop Gregory of Nin by Mestrović (1883-1962).
   (b) *Zagreb*. The Stone Gate.

6. *The Creators of 'The First Yugoslavia'*. King Alexander and Pašić during the First World War.

vinces of the new state were virtually non-existent, apart from the main trunk-route from Ljubljana to Zagreb, Belgrade, and Skopje. No railway connected Croatia with the Dalmatian coast until 1925, when the line from Zagreb to Split was opened. Even now, at the time of writing, the factories of Montenegro and Herzegovina—two regions in which there has been a valuable economic advance in the last ten years—are served only by a narrow-gauge line from Sarajevo down the Neretva Valley to Gruz, the modern port of Dubrovnik. At last however, two standard-gauge railways are being constructed in this part of Yugoslavia. Both lines, from Sarajevo to Ploce on the coast, and from Belgrade to Bar (a small port due for modernization), will from their inception be electrified. This development will overcome one of the long-term weaknesses of the Yugoslav system of communications. It should, perhaps, be added that the poor condition of Yugoslavia's roads delayed for many years the use of lorries for the long-distance transport of goods. Nowadays, with the improvement of road surfaces, it is no longer so unusual to meet a lorry crawling slowly up towards the Austrian frontier and the network of Europe's motorways.

Agriculture still remains the primary occupation of the Yugoslavs, despite the considerable growth of industry in the nineteen-fifties. In 1961 57.3 per cent. of the actual working population was employed in farming, even though there has been a marked drift of the population away from the land and into the new industries since the bad harvests of 1950 and 1952. About a fifth of the land-surface of Yugoslavia consists of soil upon which crops are grown. Most of this arable land is given up to the cultivation of cereals. Wheat is the most extensive crop, but, even so, the Yugoslavs do not grow enough for their own needs. The only year since the war in which there has been a bumper harvest of wheat was 1959. A higher yield comes from the cultivation of maize, and Yugoslavia and Roumania compete for first place among the maize producers of Europe. Barley, oats, and rye are also cultivated in the same regions. Vegetables, cattle fodder, and industrial crops occupy a much smaller area than cereals; between them they take up the equivalent of less than half the land devoted to wheat alone. Nevertheless, hemp and sugar-beet and tobacco provide some of the less fertile districts with local industries. There are tobacco factories at Mostar (Herzegovina), Sarajevo and Banja Luka (Bosnia), Skopje (Macedonia), and Titograd (Montenegro). There are considerable fruit-growing areas along the major rivers and over the lower hills, as well as in the coastal belt. Two-thirds of the fruit trees in the country are plums. This predominance of the plum-tree is especially marked in Slovenia, northern Bosnia, and western Serbia. It is these regions that produce the national drink, *šljivovica,* a latently potent plum-brandy, deceptively innocuous in appearance. Vineyards cover almost as much arable land as fruit-trees, and most parts of the country produce local wines, some of good quality. Yugoslavia is among

FIG. 1: OCCUPATIONS OF THE YUGOSLAV
WORKERS, 1961.

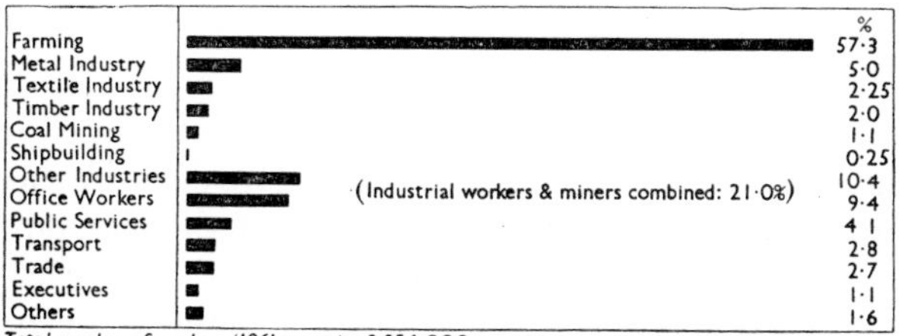

| | | % |
|---|---|---|
| Farming | | 57·3 |
| Metal Industry | | 5·0 |
| Textile Industry | | 2·25 |
| Timber Industry | | 2·0 |
| Coal Mining | | 1·1 |
| Shipbuilding | | 0·25 |
| Other Industries | (Industrial workers & miners combined: 21·0%) | 10·4 |
| Office Workers | | 9·4 |
| Public Services | | 4·1 |
| Transport | | 2·8 |
| Trade | | 2·7 |
| Executives | | 1·1 |
| Others | | 1·6 |

*Total number of workers (1961 census) : 8.354.000*

the top ten of the world's wine-producing countries; the white wines of Slovenia and the deep red wines of Dalmatia have in the last decade become so well-known abroad that over a million bottles were sold in Britain alone in one year.

The Serbs have been great producers and exporters of pigs and cattle for centuries. Sixty years ago it was possible for Austria-Hungary to put political pressure on Serbia by manipulating the tariffs against Serbian livestock; even in the nineteen-thirties a quarter of Yugoslavia's total exports consisted of pigs and cattle, alive or slaughtered. Animals now play a less important rôle

FIG. 2: INDUSTRIALIZATION:
OCCUPATIONAL CHANGES

(The dark column indicates the percentage of the actual working population engaged in Agriculture. The white column indicates the percentage engaged in Industry, Mining and Transport.)

1931 census — 71·2% / 12·3%
1953 census — 68·3% / 18·8%
1961 census — 57·3% / 23·8%

FIG. 3: UTILIZATION OF LAND-SURFACE
IN YUGOSLAVIA

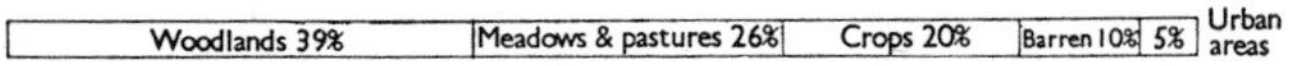

| Woodlands 39% | Meadows & pastures 26% | Crops 20% | Barren 10% | 5% | Urban areas |

in the economy, although they continue to figure on any list of the principal articles of export. The Voivodina has, like neighbouring Hungary, specialized in horse-breeding; today it is one of the most densely horse-populated regions in Europe. The annual spring agricultural Fair in Novi Sad, the capital of the Voivodina, attracts many more domestic exhibitors than the eight Trade Fairs held elsewhere in the country, perhaps because it still retains more than a suggestion of a rodeo. Official statistics show that a quarter of the entire land surface of Yugoslavia remains given over to meadows or to pastures.

The same statistics indicate that two-fifths of Yugoslavia is still covered by forests. In wealth of woodland Yugoslavia ranks fourth in Europe. Although nearly a half of these forests consist of low trees or brushwood, there is a considerable timber industry, especially in Slovenia. Official policy in recent years has sought to encourage preservation of some sections of this forest land, and there has in consequence been a reduction in the amount of felled timber, but new roads are being constructed to open up untouched tracts of woodland. When this is done, the timber industry—which in 1959 was behind only the metal and textile industries in numbers of men employed—should recover its importance.

Nearly one-tenth of the land surface consists of barren mountains or marshland; it must, therefore, for purposes of agriculture or forestry, be reckoned as unproductive. Some of the mountains, however, contain rich mineral deposits, and one of the most spectacular developments of the Yugoslav economy in the last ten years has been the utilization of this valuable source of industrial wealth. Even in the nineteen-thirties Yugoslavia was producing a tenth of the world's supply of bauxite and a twentieth of the world's supply of lead from deposits in the Dinaric Alps. In those days, however, the bauxite was exported for processing into aluminium in other countries. By harnessing the mountain streams the Yugoslavs have now brought electrical power to the bauxite deposits, and are rapidly turning some of the remoter regions of Dalmatia, Herzegovina, and Montenegro into one of the most important sources of aluminium in Europe. Yugoslavia continues to hold a high place among Europe's producers of lead, zinc, copper, chromium, and antimony. Nine new lead and zinc mines have been opened since the war, to tap the deposits of Kosmet and Macedonia. The output of these ores has increased threefold on the 1939 figure. Bor, in eastern Serbia near the Bulgarian frontier, has the largest copper mine in Europe. Uranium ore has recently been discovered in Bosnia.

There are large coal deposits in Bosnia, Serbia, and Slovenia, but although it is extensively mined it is of negligible value, since only 5 per cent. is good quality hard coal. There is a rapidly expanding iron and steel industry in the northern half of Yugoslavia with extensive works at Ženica (Bosnia), Sišak (Croatia), and Celje and Jesenice (Slovenia). A large steelworks is to be built in the next few years down in Macedonia, near Skopje; a £28 million contract for the construction work was given to two British companies at the end of 1962. Yugoslav steel production has already increased six times over since before the war and is greater than any of the other countries of south-eastern Europe, but it remains small by western European standards, only one-tenth the output of France or one-thirteenth the output of Britain.

The Yugoslavs are proud not only of their increased steel production, but also of the growth of the petroleum industry. There was a small yield of crude oil before the war, but in the last decade new sources of supply have been opened up in Slavonia (between the Sava and Drava rivers) and refineries have been built in Bosnia. The oil refining capacity is now fourteen times as great as it was before the war, while the production of petroleum has increased to nearly a thousand times the 1939 figure. Even so, the actual output is still not enough for Yugoslavia's own requirements, but the industry makes rapid advances each year and there are considerable untapped reserves. Capital expenditure on both the steel and the petroleum industries has been high—much of it under credit arrangements made with the U.S.A. in the early nineteen-fifties—and the Yugoslavs are acutely conscious of the need to push up productivity in both these branches of the economy.

The textile industry is spread fairly evenly throughout the country and employs a high proportion of the labour force, but it depends extensively on the import of raw materials. In this respect the close political links between Yugoslavia and the United Arab Republic have a particular significance, since the U.A.R. is the fifth largest exporter of cotton in the world. On the other hand, local resources are utilized for the chemical industry and for the manufacture of electrical equipment, and all the principal Yugoslav towns have plant specializing in these two branches of the economy. The shipbuilding industry has assumed importance in recent years and preparations are being made for its further expansion. There are good shipyards in Split, Pula, and Rijeka. The Split yards can already build vessels up to 22,000 tons and are being extended to construct 70,000-ton tankers. The industry will almost certainly play a major rôle in Yugoslavia's drive for more exports. In 1962 the yards were building vessels of more than 10,000 tons displacement for American, Argentinian, and Brazilian companies, as well as for the Yugoslav merchant fleet.

The rapid industrialization has been assisted by the development of extensive hydro-electric schemes, which have made it possible for factories to be opened in previously remote mountain areas. The hydro-electric centre at Mavrovo, near the Albanian frontier in Macedonia, is the most ambitious plant in the Balkans, and the Jablanica system has brought electricity to the wild regions of Herzegovina. In May 1962 the largest hydro-electric plant of all was opened near Split; it harnesses the waters of the River Cetina. The electrical supplies in the different parts of the country used to fluctuate with changing water levels. To counteract this the power plants throughout the country have been connected by a grid system, and it is therefore possible for the melting of the winter snow of the Slovene regions to meet shortages which occur in the dry summer season further south. The hydro-electric scheme has not only encouraged industry to spread itself more widely; it has also improved the standard of living in the more backward regions. Over a third of the villages can now receive electricity throughout the year, a remarkably high level for this part of Europe. Of course, the degree of electrification varies throughout the country as a whole. By 1960 four out of every five farms in Slovenia received electricity, but in Bosnia-Herzegovina and Montenegro the proportion was still less than one in five. Progress is also being made on electrifying the railways, especially in Slovenia.

In 1959, for the first time ever, industry and mining accounted for more than half of the national income of Yugoslavia. Twenty years earlier it had been less than a fifth. Actual industrial production was four times as high in 1959 as it had been in 1939. This transformation is all the more remarkable in view of the ravages of the war years, when two-fifths of the industrial equipment in the country was destroyed and one-third of the skilled workers killed or seriously incapacitated.

Immediately after the war the communist government nationalized all the means of industrial production and prepared master-plans for the development of the economy. There have subsequently been four main stages of industrial expansion. Initially, industry was re-started with the assistance of United Nations Reconstruction loans. The second stage was reached in 1947, when the Yugoslavs began to put into effect their First Five-Year Plan. This Plan aimed at extending the existing industries, rather than introducing new ones. It depended for success upon considerable help (financial and managerial) from the Soviet Union, and it looked for markets in Russia and the other satellite states. The breach with Russia in 1948 severely hampered the realization of the Plan, since it meant the withdrawal of Russian experts, the cessation of monetary aid, the closing of the newly established markets, and, in addition, an alarming and unforeseen jump in defence expenditure. By 1951 many of the objectives of the Plan had been abandoned, and Yugoslavia had entered the third stage of its post-war development, a period of some five years in which the country was largely dependent upon aid and credits from the U.S.A. Conditions had begun to improve by 1953, and during the following six years the pace of Yugoslavia's economic development was more rapid than that of any other European country except Western Germany. The fourth stage of expansion has been marked by the adoption of a Second Five-Year Plan (1957-61). Although this Plan was more concerned with agriculture than with industry, it included provision for huge grants from the central government to help the industrialization of the more backward regions of

Kosmet and Macedonia. In this respect the Plan has had a marked success. Developments since 1961 suggest that long-term schemes are being replaced by annual plans— a modification of the system which probably reflects both uncertainty about export markets and doubts over the continuance of American credit.

While industrial output has made astounding progress, agricultural production has remained uneven and unpredictable. It has been severely hit by bad droughts (and consequently disastrous harvests) in several years, notably in 1952, when production of grain actually fell to less than half the average annual yield in the nineteen-thirties. Not all of the privations can be blamed on nature; the extent of the failure was increased by sheer mismanagement and, above all, by the folly of enforced collectivization. When Churchill first met Tito in August 1944 he advised him not to collectivize the farms after the war on the Russian model, since this was likely to increase peasant hostility. Despite this gratuitous advice—which was, perhaps, resented—much farmland was collectivized during the three years of Yugoslav subservience to Russia. Even after the breach of 1948 this policy was continued, partly because the Yugoslavs were anxious to prove to the world that, despite their ideological differences with Stalin, they remained good Marxists. Measures against recalcitrant peasants were actually stiffer in 1949 than in the previous two years, and by 1950 one-fifth of the total cultivated acreage had been given over to collective farms.

Huge farms were not, however, suited to the nature of the Yugoslav terrain, and the imposition on the countryside of a regiment of Party officials aroused resentment among the stubbornly individualistic peasantry. In the spring of 1950 there were riots against collectivization in parts of Croatia, but the Government persisted in its policy until the calamitous harvest of 1952. In March 1953 Edvard Kardelj, Tito's principal political lieutenant, admitted in a speech that enforced collectivization had been an error. Yugoslav small-holders were thereupon given greater freedom, although they were encouraged to collaborate in agrarian co-operatives. By 1960 88 per cent. of the agricultural land had once again been divided into individual smallhold-ings (average size, 11½ acres), but more than half of the peasant population was associated with co-operative enterprises. There is, of course, much that the peasant can gain from a co-operative—chemical fertilizers, machinery, and expert advice, for example—and it is clear that this 'socialist sector of the agricultural economy', as it is called, has had much better results than the independent peasants, who still cultivate their strips of land with primitive equipment.

The Second Five-Year Plan put particular stress on the introduction of modern techniques in the socialist sector; it aimed at pushing up the rate of agricultural produc-tion by 7 per cent. in each of the years 1957-61. In 1959 a record grain crop enabled the Yugoslav Government to dispense with wheat imports for the first time since the establishment of the Republic. The harvests of 1960 and 1961, although good by the standards of ten years earlier, were still not adequate for Yugoslavia's needs, and the Yugoslavs again had to purchase wheat from the United States.

After the near-disasters of the First Five-Year Plan and the collectivization of agriculture, the Yugoslavs have avoided a slavish copying of Soviet methods. They claim to have evolved a unique type of Socialism, which retains some of the stimulus of competition from the (to them) discredited system of private enterprise. Some of their critics maintain that the Yugoslav system is not even Socialist; and it is certainly true that during 1961 and 1962 Yugoslav communist publications (and, indeed, Tito's own speeches) have shown some alarm at the decline of what they call 'Socialist morality' in business dealings. Nevertheless, if the cardinal principle of Socialism is the management by the State and for the community of the means of production, distribution, and exchange, then there cannot be much doubt about the character of the Yugoslav economy. It does, however, clearly possess greater adaptability and elasticity than the Soviet system.

The Yugoslav variation on the Socialist theme was primarily the work of a remarkable economist, Boris Kidrić, a trained chemist and the son of a Slovene professor. He became director of the Yugoslav Economic Council in 1947, after four exacting years fighting as a Partisan in Slovenia, and by the time he died in 1953 (exhausted by overwork at the age of forty-one) he had revolutionized the management of industry and agriculture. Partly as a result of the frustrations in the First Five-Year Plan, Kidrić made economic decentralization a key feature of his policy, and this principle has been followed ever since 1950. Within a general plan determined by the Federal Government and amplified by the governments of the six republics, the workers in an individual factory or enterprise decide on the character and extent of production. They also have to take decisions to ensure the effective marketing of their products; and they thus find themselves competing with other State concerns which are seeking to secure orders. Should the enterprise make a profit, some of it will be shared out as a bonus to the workers. Should it make a loss, the workers' earnings are cut. Should it continue to show a deficit over a long period of time, the State would withdraw subsidies, and it would be forced to close down, its workers thus becoming unemployed.

The basic units of this system are the Workers' Councils, which were authorized by the Law of Workers' Management of June 1950, although some had been established in the previous year as an experiment. They are self-governing bodies elected by the members of a factory or collective each year; there are some 13,000 Workers' Councils in the country as a whole. Each Council, in its turn, elects representatives to sit on the Board of Management, which also contains nominated directors and expert advisers. The Board determines details of production and the distribution of profits, but its decisions have to be accepted by the Workers' Council before they are implemented. The Workers' Council has responsibility not only for the business operations of the enterprise, but also for many of the social services of the community (adult education, cultural activities, sports clubs, holiday centres, etc.). Naturally, smaller enterprises have fewer amenities; and, indeed, where a factory employs less than thirty people, all the workers together form the Council. In the bigger concerns particular care is taken to make the composition of the Councils representative of all the employees. Thus nearly one in six of the members of the Councils are between the ages of eighteen and twenty-five. Actual factory-workers or miners (as opposed to office-staff) form three-quarters of the membership. About a sixth of the members are women.

The Yugoslav authorities attach great importance to this system of workers' management. They maintain that it represents the achievement of the early Socialist ideal of 'handing over the factories to the workers', and that it completes the transformation of Yugoslavia into an economic democracy. Outsiders remain a little sceptical. The disputes that get reported in the Yugoslav Press often seem to have a familiar ring. In December 1961, for example, there was a conflict between the Board of Management and the Workers' Council at the electrical equipment factory in Čačak, a small town in Central Serbia, over distribution of an additional bonus to the 'most deserving workers'. At the same time the newspapers were reporting a meeting attended by the employees of a Belgrade furniture factory which had expressed a vote of no confidence in the Workers' Council, since, allegedly, it had carried out the wishes of the Director and not of the people who had elected it. Editorial comment on these and other episodes suggest that there is some disquiet at the distribution of earnings in the various enterprises; but it would of course be rash to generalize from isolated cases. There is obviously at times a certain resentment at the minor privileges given to members of the Workers' Councils. The official reply to such criticism is that the members of the councils were elected in the first instance for only one year (although, of course, they can be re-elected, and more than a third are), and that in time all the efficient workers will have an opportunity of serving on the Council. In the first ten years of the Councils' existence one in twenty-five of the Yugoslav population was elected to serve on them. The Workers' Councils are thus both a method of encouraging a sense of public responsibility and a means of political education. We shall have to return to this question of their general influence in the next chapter.

The standard of living of the Yugoslav worker rose

perceptibly between 1957 and 1961. Wages went up 8 per cent. and there were more goods in the shops, greater variety in the clothes, more flats, and more cars. But it is all too easy to get a misleading impression. The number of private cars did, indeed, double between 1957 and 1960, but this was largely because of the manufacture, under licence in Yugoslavia, of small Italian Fiats, rather than because of a boom in the Yugoslav automobile industry. (Buses and lorries still have to be imported.) Moreover, the number of private cars remains small by western European standards. In 1960 the Yugoslavs averaged one private car for every 340 people; the British, in the same year, had two for every 19. Similarly, although 60,000 new flats are becoming available each year in the bigger cities, there remains an acute shortage of accommodation, and more than half of those built contain only two rooms. Moreover there are frequent complaints of preferential treatment for the bigger industrial enterprises in the construction of flats. It appears that only the richer factories have sufficient profits to put down the 50 per cent. deposit that is required before a loan can be obtained from a municipal housing fund. Early in 1962 this particular grievance was taken up at the highest level in Belgrade, and it is likely that in the future there will be a more equitable system of access to the housing funds. The actual rent of a flat constitutes a large share in the individual worker's budget; and the rate was $2\frac{1}{2}$ times higher in 1961 than it had been in 1957. Nevertheless, despite these criticisms, there can be no doubt of the general improvement in living conditions, in the villages as well as in the towns, since before the war.

One problem that is not generally appreciated abroad is the rise in population. It has not, of course, been so rapid as in the nations of the Far East, but it has, none the less, been spectacular. Since the unification of the country in 1918 the population has increased at a rate comparable to that experienced in Britain during the early years of the Industrial Revolution. The accompanying diagram illustrates the development of the two countries, separated though they are by a time-lag of one hundred and twenty years. Had it not been for the crippling loss of a generation in the Second World War, the extent of increase would have been almost parallel.

FIG. 4: POPULATION INCREASE: A COMPARISON BETWEEN GREAT BRITAIN IN THE EARLY NINE-TEENTH CENTURY AND YUGOSLAVIA IN THE TWENTIETH

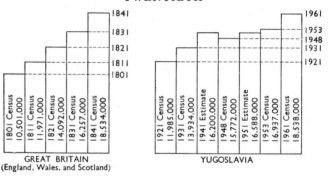

Provided that there are no more disasters in the next twenty years, the population of Yugoslavia should, by 1985, be double that of 1918. The chief effect of this increase has been on agriculture: more mouths eat more bread. It is also true that the Yugoslavs now expect higher quality food than the subsistence rations on which the mass of the peasantry kept alive before the war. An increase in agricultural production remains a high priority for Yugoslavia's planners if they are to avoid discontent at home.

The Yugoslav Government must, however, be primarily concerned with another pressing problem, the future of foreign trade. For here the balance-sheet looks sombre. In each of the four years 1957-60 Yugoslavia had a total adverse trade balance of between seventy and eighty thousand million dinars; that is to say, each year the value of Yugoslavia's imports came to between £33 and £39 million more than the country's exports. In proportion to the extent of the national income, this is a higher deficit than most other European countries have experienced in recent years. But the figures for 1961 were even more alarming. Imports rose in value by 9 per cent. while exports fell by 2 per cent., and, in consequence, Yugoslavia had an adverse trade balance of some £51 million. Although, subsequently, an agreement with Russia to settle outstanding debts reduced this amount by some £5 million, it remains the worst deficit in the country's history.

Yugoslav economists have stressed the importance of three reasons, in particular, for this deficit: the rising cost of heavy capital equipment, which is still needed to increase the future industrial output of the country; the persistent drain on Yugoslavia's resources of repaying foreign loans, originally negotiated to assist industrialization in the early nineteen-fifties; and a complicated reform in the system of international exchange which reduced the purchasing-power abroad of the dinar, the Yugoslav unit of currency. Yet, as the economists themselves have implied, there are two more basic explanations. One of these we have mentioned already—the failure of agricultural output to keep pace with industry, and the necessity to import basic foodstuffs. The second reason becomes clear if we study the pattern of Yugoslav trade with other countries.

Table I (p. 83) provides a comparison of Yugoslavia's trade relations with certain countries in two groups of two years each, separated by a quarter of a century. The particular dates (1934-35 and 1959-60) were chosen because they were, in a sense, 'normal' years: after 1935 the Germans increased political pressure until they gained a disproportionate share of the foreign trade; and it is not yet possible to make a final assessment of changes since 1960. Unfortunately, it is also impossible to give accurate comparisons of the value of individual items of export for these two periods, since they are shown in present-day statistics under different categories from the pre-war statistics. Estimates can, however, be made in general terms.

In 1934-35 Yugoslavia was still subject to the trade conditions which had predominated before the First World War. Despite tariff barriers, more than two-fifths of the exports and about a third of the imports went to, or came from, the lands that had formed the Austro-Hungarian Empire, while a further sixth of the foreign trade was with Germany, the other country which had 'opened up the Balkans' at the end of the nineteenth century. Three-quarters of Yugoslavia's exports were, in fact, delivered within a radius of 700 miles from Belgrade, while the only sizeable imports from outside that area came from Britain (mainly heavy industrial goods) and the U.S.A. (mainly cotton). There was virtually no trade with the Soviet Union—with whom, indeed, the Yugoslavs had no diplomatic relations until 1940. The export of livestock was the chief source of revenue for Yugoslavia in this period, followed by timber, and wheat, and maize.

## TABLE I

COMPARISON OF THE DISTRIBUTION OF YUGO-
SLAV FOREIGN TRADE OVER TWENTY-FIVE YEARS
(ANNUAL AVERAGES OF PERCENTAGE OF VALUE OF TRADE)

| COUNTRY | 1934-35 | | 1959-60 | |
|---|---|---|---|---|
| | Exports to | Imports from | Exports to | Imports from |
| Austria | 15·4 | 12·2 | 4·5 | 4·1 |
| Czechoslovakia | 12·4 | 12·9 | 4·0 | 3·3 |
| France | 1·5 | 4·6 | 2·0 | 2·8 |
| Germany | 17·0 | 15·0 | Western 9·3 | 14·5 |
| | | | Eastern 6·9 | 4·3 |
| Greece | 4·2 | 1·3 | 4·0 | 0·9 |
| Hungary | 4·5 | 4·0 | 4·2 | 3·4 |
| Italy | 18·6 | 12·3 | 12·7 | 11·5 |
| Poland | 1·4 | 1·7 | 5·6 | 3·9 |
| Turkey | 0·1 | 0·1 | 0·4 | 0·4 |
| U.A.R. (Egypt & Syria) | Figures not available but trade very slight. | | 3·3 | 4·2 |
| United Kingdom | 5·0 | 9·7 | 7·4 | 5·4 |
| U.S.A. | 4·9 | 6·3 | 6·7 | 15·5 |
| U.S.S.R. | 0·0 | 0·01 | 9·8 | 7·7 |
| Other countries (including Egypt in 1934-35 figs.) | 15·0 | 19·9 | 19·2 | 18·1 |
| Total annual average value (at 1959 prices & exchange rates.) | £40 mil. | £36 mil. | £78·3 mil. | £113·7 mil. |

## TABLE II

YUGOSLAV TRADE WITH THE COMMON MARKET
COUNTRIES, 1959-1961

| | Percentage value of EXPORTS | Percentage value of IMPORTS |
|---|---|---|
| 1959 | 26·2 | 28·1 |
| 1960 | 25·6 | 32·1 |
| 1961 | 24·6 | 38·5 |

Twenty-five years later, livestock and animal-products
(such as hides and leather) remain high on the list of
exports, but first place is held by small manufactured
goods, and there has also been a substantial rise in the
quantity of non-ferrous metals sent abroad. Maize is

still exported; wheat imported. The pattern of trade has been substantially modified, but not to such an extent as the changes in the Yugoslav economy would lead one to expect. There has been a marked falling-away in trade with Austria and Czechoslovakia, but, despite the troubled politics of the intervening years, Germany and Italy and Hungary still hold much the same position in the Table. Nearly a half of Yugoslavia's exports continue to be delivered within 700 miles of Belgrade. The two biggest differences from the inter-war period come, as one might expect, from trade with the two master Powers, Russia and America, and from trade with the 'unaligned nations' of Asia and, to a lesser extent, Africa. There has, for example, been a substantial increase in trade with Egypt; but although Yugoslavia's cotton may now come from the Nile Valley rather than from the Deep South, this has been offset as a dollar-saving device by the need to import American agricultural surpluses.

The significance of this problem of the geographical distribution of Yugoslavia's trade may be further seen from Table II. In January 1959 the six Common Market countries (Germany, Italy, France, Belgium, Holland, and Luxembourg) made their first cuts in import duties paid by the member-states in trading with each other. Further annual cuts followed, and the process will be continued until 1966, when it is assumed that there will no longer be any trade barriers between the six countries. The effect of these tariff-cuts has, of course, been to make trade between the six members much easier and more profitable at the expense of other countries outside the Common Market. Yugoslavia, as a non-member, has felt the full burden of this development because of her extensive trade with both Western Germany and Italy.

At the risk of over-simplification, it could be said that, by the end of 1961, the Yugoslavs were earning almost 2/6d in each £1 less for their exports to the Common Market countries and were paying 7/- in each £1 more for their imports. The Common Market was thus of fundamental importance in increasing the Yugoslav trade deficit of 1961. And these figures, it should be emphasized, apply only to trade with the original six members. It is not surprising that the Yugoslavs are watching the attitude of other countries to the Common Market with some anxiety.

Clearly the Common Market poses a major problem for Yugoslavia, and one that calls for an urgent solution. As a communist state, Yugoslavia cannot herself become a member of the European Economic Community (as the Common Market should be called), for it is an organization which is intended to further the political integration of Europe, and not merely economic collaboration. The Yugoslavs must, accordingly, turn away from their traditional trading areas and increase their commercial links with the Soviet bloc and with the Asian and African countries.

With each stage in the growth of the Common Market, so exports and imports between Yugoslavia and the Soviet Union have increased in value. In 1961 trade between the two countries was 70 per cent. higher than in 1960; in 1962 an agreement was signed to increase it by 58 per cent. on the 1961 figures. The Yugoslavs themselves are not particularly happy about this development. They complain that the Russians are inclined to be slow in making foreign exchange earnings available; and they also complain, from experience, that Russian machinery has a short life, and that there are long delays in securing spare parts. Their greatest fear is that increased trade with Russia will limit their country's political independence, and they are determined at all costs to avoid complete reliance on the Soviet bloc. At the time of writing it looks as if by the end of 1963 two-fifths of Yugoslav trade will be with the Soviet Union and her allies in the Warsaw Pact. By 1965 trade with Poland alone should be as great as it was with Russia in 1960.

The Yugoslavs have also been looking for markets outside Europe. There has been a significant increase in commercial links with Latin America, but it is more probable that the Yugoslavs will increase their earnings from the African and Middle Eastern countries. Early in 1962 President Tito visited Egypt and the Sudan in the hope of encouraging trade exchanges and economic co-operation between the unaligned countries. In this respect the experience that the Yugoslavs have gained in engineering technique and building methods is likely to prove of particular value. Thus between January 1958 and December 1961 Yugoslav engineers undertook the construction of Ethiopia's first modern port, at Assab on the Eritrean coast. At the same time harbour installations were being erected at three towns in Syria, and preliminary work was being done on a ten-year project to drain the Salt Lakes near Calcutta and to construct a new town on the reclaimed land.

In the inter-war years it would have been out of the question for any Yugoslav organization to be offered contracts for this type of work by a foreign government. It was, of course, the other way round: thus, to take only one example, the first hydro-electric works in Dalmatia were constructed in the late nineteen-twenties by Italians and developed further by the French. This change is a sign of the economic advance since 1945. There are still plenty of headaches for the expert planners sitting in the State Secretariat of National Economy in Belgrade; as we have seen, some are forced on them from outside, such as the questions raised by the Common Market; others result from failures at home, most notably in agriculture. Yet, despite all the limitations on development that we have noticed, the long-term prospect is not discouraging. Much must depend on the balance-sheet of the years 1963-66. There has, unquestionably, been an economic revolution as well as a political revolution in Yugoslavia—but, in this case, it is a revolution that is not yet completed.

# 4

## TODAY AND TOMORROW

ALTHOUGH THE ECONOMIC difficulties discussed in
the last chapter were among the most serious problems facing the Yugoslav Government in the course
of 1962, there were plenty of other questions calling for
solution. Indeed in many respects 1962 was the year of
greatest change since the breach with the other communist countries in 1948. Revision of the Constitution
so as to ensure continuation of the Yugoslav type of
socialism and the peaceful succession of new leaders was
high on the list of priorities. So also was the closely
related problem of permitting more self-government
and greater freedom of expression without endangering
the existing system, which (naturally enough, from their
point of view) the Yugoslav communists have every
intention of retaining. And then, too, there were urgent
questions of foreign policy, prompted partly by shifts
in the balance of world power and partly by tension
among communist rivals. All these topics will be considered in this final chapter.

The Yugoslav Press gave greatest attention among
these problems to the Constitution, and it is this subject
which we shall consider first. All countries which have
experienced a violent political revolution have their
machinery of government regulated by a written constitution, a device unfamiliar to the British people for
over three hundred years. In some states, such as the
U.S.A., the Constitution is an almost sacred document,
amended from time to time but with its fundamental

assumptions unchallenged. Other lands, however, have changed their constitutions with much greater rapidity; and it is to this category that Yugoslavia belongs. There were two constitutions in the twenty years between the wars and there have been three constitutional laws since the establishment of the Republic.

The fundamental Republican Constitution was, as we have seen, proclaimed in 1946 and was based on the Soviet Constitution of ten years previously. The country was divided into six republics, with Kosmet and the Voivodina forming self-governing provinces within Serbia. Each of the six republics had an Assembly responsible for regional affairs, but all national questions were decided by the Federal Assembly (parliament) and the Federal Government in Belgrade. Effective power was in the hands of the Presidium, a kind of cabinet headed by a prime minister (Tito). There was a President of the Republic (i.e. of the whole of Yugoslavia), but he was little more than a figurehead.

The 1946 Constitution was substantially modified in January 1953. There were two main reasons for making alterations at this date: the Yugoslavs wished to demonstrate their independence of the Soviet pattern of government; and they wanted to write into the Constitution the system of Workers' Councils which, as we noticed in the last chapter, began to regulate the economic life of the local communities in 1950. The Constitutional Law of 1953 accordingly changed the character both of government and of parliament. The Presidium was replaced as a cabinet by a Federal Executive Council, which elected a President who was to serve both as Head of State and as prime minister. Marshal Tito was duly elected to this office, thereby attaining a position similar to that held by the President of the

U.S.A. As his deputies Tito had four Vice-Presidents, officially equal in status. At the same time, the Constitutional Law also provided for one of the two chambers in the parliament to be elected by the workers in the state enterprises.

In December 1960 the authorities announced that work was to start on the preparation of yet another constitution. Officially it was intended that this document would show the progress which had been made in the preceding eight years in reducing the authority of the State and in encouraging the growth of 'socialist democracy'. Foreign observers interpreted the decision to modify the Constitution as acceptance of the fact that President Tito was an old man and that there was no obvious successor who possessed his extraordinary shrewdness, ability, and personality. Clearly the legal experts ran into difficulties in drawing up the new statute for it was not presented to the Assembly until the end of September 1962, eight months behind schedule. It was then extensively discussed and slightly modified, and duly became law in April 1963.

The 1962 proposals outlined what must be the most complicated political system in Europe. Sections on the rights and duties of the citizens were carried over from earlier constitutions. The six republics and the two autonomous provinces within Serbia were retained, but in order to symbolize the progress that had been made in the previous decade, the official name of the country was changed from 'Federal People's Republic of Yugoslavia' to 'Federal Socialist Republic of Yugoslavia'. All this looks relatively straightforward; the difficulties come when we examine the structure of government.

Figure 5 shows the method which it was proposed to embody in the 1963 Constitutional Law. We will examine

# FIG. 5: THE STRUCTURE OF GOVERNMENT IN YUGOSLAVIA

## CONSTITUTIONAL LAW OF 1963

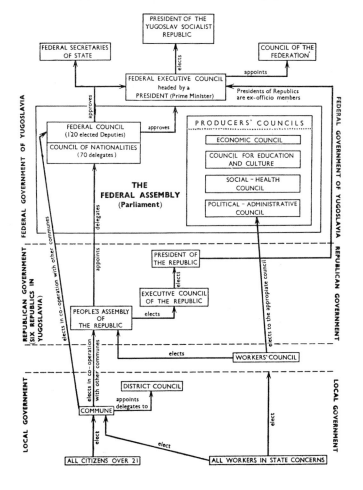

the proposals starting from the bottom of the diagram. In presenting the new scheme to the Assembly, Vice-President Kardelj stressed the importance of the local councils of the communes as the basic political unit in the land. There are at present some 800 communes in Yugoslavia, each representing on the average 18,000 adult citizens. The communes are controlled by councils of fifteen to twenty men and women who sit in two bodies, one of which is directly elected by everyone over the age of twenty-one and the other by all workers in state organizations, whether industrial, agricultural or professional. Hence the workers in a nationalized undertaking vote for both parts of the communal council, but the self-employed worker or the peasant who farms his own land only votes for the council of citizens. This distinction between the rights of workers in 'the socialized sector of the economy' and in private enterprise is maintained throughout the political framework.

The new Constitutional Law proposes that the communal councillors should not only supervise local affairs through a District Council (as, for example, a U.D.C. does in Britain) but should unite with half a dozen neighbouring councils of communes to form a constituency and elect representatives to sit in one of the six republican regional assemblies and deputies to sit in one of the chambers of parliament in Belgrade. This Federal Assembly (parliament) consists of two parts: the Federal Council, where the constituency deputies sit; and four specialized councils of producers who are elected by the Workers' Councils (the composition of which we examined in Chapter Three). These four new bodies are called the Economic Council, the Council for Education and Culture, the Social-Health Council and the Political-Administrative Council. It would of course be extremely cumbersome to have a five-chamber parliament, and this is not the intention of the Constitution. All proposed legislation will be considered by the Federal Council and will then, before becoming law, be referred to whichever of the four Councils is the appropriate one for the subject under discussion. Thus a proposal to raise the school-leaving age would be considered by the Federal Council and the Council for Education and Culture, and a proposal to increase the number of sanatoria by the Federal Council and the Social-Health Council. The authors of the new Constitution maintain that this system has the advantage of permitting questions to be discussed both by the political organizations of the citizens and by the elected experts in the specialized bodies, forming what Kardelj described as 'a kind of supreme Workers' Council'.

The electoral system looks strange to those of us accustomed to the British type of voting procedure. The same method is used in choosing representatives for both the Federal Assembly and the assemblies of the six republics, but for the sake of simplicity we will concern ourselves here only with the Federal Assembly. We will look first at the Federal Council. Meetings of citizens are held in the various communes to propose possible candidates. The communal councils then choose one or more names from the list of candidates submitted to them. The names of the chosen representatives are then referred back to the individual citizens who vote, in secret, for or against the candidate (if there is only one) or choose one of the candidates selected by the communes (if there is more than one). Once a candidate has a clear majority he is formally elected by the communal councils. The new Federal Council will comprise 120 members elected in this way, each deputy representing

on the average some 120,000 adult citizens (by comparison, a British M.P. rarely has more than 60,000 electors
in his constituency). There are also 70 deputies in the
Federal Council appointed by the assemblies of the six
republics and the two autonomous provinces. They form
the Council of Nationalities, a body which only meets
if there are disputes between the six republics. At other
times the delegates to the Council of Nationalities automatically sit in the Federal Council with the elected
members.

Each of the four producers' councils in the Federal
Assembly also consists of 120 members, but they are
elected by a slightly different method. Candidates are
nominated by the workers at general meetings and their
names are submitted to the Workers' Council which
then chooses one person from the list submitted to it
without referring the selection back to the workers
themselves. Since there are more than 13,000 Workers'
Councils and provision is made for only 480 parliamentary representatives, it is obvious that the smaller
concerns must amalgamate with similar undertakings
in their locality for purposes of election. Of course, the
successful candidate sits in whichever of the four
councils is appropriate to his occupation; for example,
hospitals would elect to the Social-Health Council and
factories to the Economic Council. Members of these
four councils get only their expenses paid, as they are
still considered to be productive workers rather than
politicians; deputies in the Federal Council have a
regular salary. Representatives in both the Federal
Council and the specialist councils hold office for four
years, but are divided into two groups so that half the
places in the Assembly come up for election every
other year.

If we now look at the top of Figure 5 we will see that there are also changes on the executive side of the Government. The American-type Presidency introduced in 1953 is abolished, and so too are the four Vice-Presidents; there is once again to be a figurehead President of the Republic, who will be assisted by one Vice-President. The President appoints the prime minister ('President of the Federal Executive Council') who is the effective head of the Government. He in turn submits a list of ministers and other cabinet members to the Federal Council, which has the right to accept or reject the nominations. The ministers ('Federal Secretaries of State') are automatically members of the Federal Executive Council, and so too are the Presidents of the six republics, but there will also be some members of the cabinet who are free from departmental responsibilities. A new 'Council of the Federation' is set up; this appears to be a kind of Privy Council of distinguished politicians and it would meet only occasionally, mainly at moments of crisis. (For example, the Council of the Federation would seek to settle disagreements between the President of the Republic and the President of the Federal Executive Council if these should arise.)

The new Constitution is intended to permit a larger number of citizens to take part in government at various levels. It accordingly limits the members of the councils (and indeed many of the members of the Government) to holding their particular office for only four years, although in some instances they may be re-elected for a further four years. The President of the Republic may hold office for only two terms (eight years), but the Constitution explicitly states that this prohibition shall not apply to President Tito 'owing to his historical merits in the construction of the Republic'.

There is much that is unusual and interesting in this new constitutional scheme and it should not be dismissed as elaborate window-dressing, as some commentators have suggested. We have examined it in considerable detail because the Yugoslavs hope that it will not only meet their social and political requirements, but will serve as an example of a modern 'progressive' constitution for other socialist states to follow.

There are five main differences between the revolutionary socialism of Yugoslavia and the orthodox Marxism of Russia and China. One of these differences concerns foreign policy; the belief that it is possible for a communist state to remain 'uncommitted' in the rivalry of East and West (a theme to which we shall return later in this chapter). Two of the differences are economic, and were noted in Chapter Three: the acceptance of a high degree of private trading outside 'the socialist sector of the economy', particularly among the peasantry; and the encouragement of competition between State enterprises. The remaining differences are constitutional: the power of the Workers' Councils within the apparatus of Government; and the increasing tendency towards regional and local decentralization. Some Yugoslavs would add that there is a sixth difference; that the Yugoslav Constitution permits the voice of the people to make itself heard to an extent that is impossible in Russia or China. Indeed, in introducing the new constitutional proposals, Vice-President Kardelj went further than this; he maintained that they were fundamentally democratic since they enabled the elector-

---

7. *The Creator of ' the Second Yugoslavia '.* Marshal Tito at his secret headquarters in Bosnia during the Second World War.

7

ate 'to participate in solving the problems of the community in a better and more direct way than in the classical parliamentary system' (of, for example, Britain). There appears on the face of it to be some justification for this claim, both because of the multiplicity of elected bodies and the comparative frequency of elections. And of course Kardelj's remarks must be seen against the background of Yugoslavia's experience of multi-party political life in the nineteen-twenties, which made a mockery of the traditional parliamentary institutions. Nevertheless, Kardelj clearly attaches a different meaning to democracy from the interpretation accepted in Britain or the U.S.A. In Western eyes much must depend upon the type of candidate nominated by the general meetings and on the motives which induce the councils to choose one candidate rather than another. Will all these representatives in fact be nominees of the Government?

Technically each candidate is independent of party, but, as Kardelj himself said later in his speech, the political organizations 'cannot be indifferent when persons are being proposed for various posts in the social-political organs'. In all probability some independently-minded representatives will indeed be returned to the Assembly—as there were in a few instances in the 1958 elections—but the system is so weighted that it must give a considerable advantage, to put it mildly, to anyone with the communist machine behind him. All the same, this virtual monopoly of political representation does not mean that the deputies will dutifully put a

8. *Leaders of the New Yugoslavia.*
   (a) Edvard Kardelj (born 1910).
   (b) Aleksandar Ranković (born 1909).
   (c) Koca Popović (born 1908).
   (d) Rodoljub Čolaković (born 1900).

rubber-stamp of acceptance on every proposal that is put before them. Not only is this contrary to Kardelj's whole line of reasoning in his speech, it is also contrary to the experience of the last parliament. Early in 1962, for example, a modification of the health service by which individual patients would have to contribute towards the cost of hospital beds and prescriptions was rejected in the Assembly; and there has been some outspoken criticism of plans for subsidizing industry in the more backward republics out of taxes from the richer North.

Naturally, there is nothing comparable to 'Her Majesty's Opposition' in the Yugoslav parliament. There are in fact only three political organizations in Yugoslavia, all of which are closely connected and which include as members more than half the population in the appropriate age-group. The most powerful of the three is the League of Communists, as the old Communist Party re-named itself at its Sixth Congress in 1952. At that time membership of the League numbered 800,000. Ten years later it was estimated to have increased to slightly under 1,200,000, a figure which would mean that about one in twelve of the population in the age-groups eligible for membership could count themselves as fully fledged communists. The League leadership has long been dominated by veterans of the Partisan War. Even as late as 1958, 84 per cent. of the delegates to the League Congress had been members of the Communist Party before the establishment of the Republic. Tito himself commented adversely on the failure to bring young blood into the movement and particular attention has been given to this problem in the last few years, but local communist leaders still cautiously accept members only from what they term 'the ideologically most advanced' groups of workers or students. Most League members graduate, as it were, from the mass general political organization known as the Socialist Alliance, a body of about seven and a half million people. Although it is not necessary to be a communist to belong to the Socialist Alliance, the League uses it as an instrument for the political education of the country as a whole. Membership is voluntary, but desirable for anyone who is anxious for social advancement. The third group is the People's Youth Organization, a specifically communist body for young men and women between fourteen and twenty-five. It has slightly under a million and a half members, of whom about a fifth also belong to the League of Communists. Great importance is attached to the work of the P.Y.O. in training the political leaders of the future; it holds about a thousand seminars a year in political education. It also provides recreational opportunities for its members and organizes youth work in school and university vacations, for example on the construction of roads.

There are, as one would expect, other organizations in the country which have political affiliations but which are primarily social in purpose—trade unions, workers' universities, women's societies to assist families with child welfare, and a Union of Disabled Veterans to help in rehabilitating the war-wounded. Naturally there are also numerous associations for artistic expression and physical culture of one form or another, just as there are in Britain. But there is one familiar part of the British social structure which is missing in Yugoslavia; there is no established Church. Of course, there are churches in every town and village but, as in all communist countries, they exist by grace of the State rather than in close association with it. The Church Question has not been acute in Yugoslavia for several years, but it could become so again and therefore requires closer analysis.

For over a century the leading communist writers of all lands have insisted that their philosophy is based on scientific principles, that there can be no life beyond death, and that religious practices are no more than a drug to keep the working millions ignorant of the realities of their existence. In most communist states there have been periods of severe religious persecution; Stalin, for example, not only terrorized the priesthood but established 'Anti-God Museums' in some of their churches. The Yugoslavs have shown greater tolerance than either the Russians or the Chinese. In Chapter One we noticed the peculiarly mixed religious heritage of the Yugoslav lands—the north predominantly Roman Catholic, the south Orthodox, with large pockets of Muslims in the centre. The Yugoslav Kingdom used to favour the Orthodox Church because that was the religion of the Serbian people, who dominated the country's politics. One might therefore have reasonably expected the Orthodox Church to have become the particular target of the communist government. But curiously enough the Orthodox religion, while suffering a certain amount of persecution, has worked much more closely with the republican authorities than either the Roman Catholics or the Muslims. The reason for this slightly unexpected development lies back in the horrifying years of inter-racial conflict during the Second World War.

It will be remembered that the Roman Catholics supported the 'Independent Croatian State' which had been set up by the Croatian fascists, the *Ustaše*. Some of the Croatian clergy participated in the forcible conversion of Orthodox believers, especially in the fringe areas of *Ustaše*-occupied land in Bosnia, a cruel policy which, it should be added, was condemned by the Vatican authorities. Thousands of Orthodox believers were massacred by the *Ustaše* and two bishops atrociously murdered. The Muslims too were favoured by the *Ustaše*, who even permitted them to build a mosque in Zagreb, a city which had never fallen to the Turks. There were two consequences of this tragic religious feud: many Orthodox priests associated themselves with the communist Partisans because they were the avowed enemies of the *Ustaše*; and the Partisans, for their part, treated prominent Catholics as war-criminals. The bitterness created by this situation lasted for many years after the war.

Most Church land was confiscated in the early days of the Republic and some of the clergy were imprisoned, including Archbishop Stepinac (as we saw in Chapter Two). The 1946 Constitution, however, formally guaranteed religious freedom, although it insisted that 'abuse of the church and religion for political purposes, and the existence of political organizations on a religious basis, are forbidden'. These provisions were incorporated in the later constitutional measures. Articles in periodicals and newspapers continued to attack the influence of the clergy and a number of churches were closed 'for want of support'. It is difficult to assess the extent to which the communists succeeded in stamping out religious belief. The 1953 Census suggests that they made remarkably little progress. Only one in eight of the seventeen million covered by the census declared that they totally rejected all religious doctrines. Of the remaining fifteen million, 48 per cent. were registered as Orthodox, 36 per cent. as Roman Catholic, 14 per cent. Muslim, and

2 per cent. as belonging to other beliefs (including various Protestant Churches and the Jewish Faith). The proportion of non-believers was much the same in all six republics, although it was nearly three times as high in the cities as in the countryside and more marked among men than women.

Since 1953 there has been considerably more co-operation between the Church and the State. This is particularly true of the Roman Catholic Church under the wise direction of Monsignor Seper, Cardinal Stepinac's successor. In September 1960 an assembly of Roman Catholic bishops in Zagreb sent a letter to the Yugoslav Government expressing readiness to work towards normal relations between Church and State, provided that the Government applied ' consistently and liberally' the constitutional guarantees on religion. Confidential talks were subsequently held between representatives of the bishops and the Federal Committee for Religious Matters, and these seem to have overcome some of the earlier friction.

Since the establishment of the Republic the Christian Churches have received over a million pounds in financial assistance from the state, a development which could never, for example, have taken place in Russia. Individual churches are now permitted to own up to twenty-five acres of land. There have also been improvements in educational facilities. Religious instruction is still prohibited in state schools, but the various Churches are allowed to open schools of their own, primarily for pupils who are intended for the priesthood. The pupils must have completed eight years at a state school before going to one of the Church schools, and a Church school may be closed on the order of a court of law if it is found to be a centre of political propaganda. The Roman

Catholics have fourteen schools, seven theological colleges, and theological faculties associated with the Universities of Zagreb and Ljubljana. The Orthodox Church has two theological colleges and a faculty associated with Belgrade University, and the Muslims have one school and a 'Higher College' in Sarajevo. There are also three small Protestant schools. Fourteen religious periodicals are permitted, most of them monthly publications. Official statistics do not give the number of pupils in the schools nor the circulation of the periodicals.

It is of course almost impossible to estimate the influence of the Churches in Yugoslavia today. Muslim traditions appear to survive in family life in Bosnia-Herzegovina and Macedonia; the little street-urchins of Skopje, for example, retain Muslim first-names, while many of their fathers and grandfathers still wear the fez. Personal observation at services in three Orthodox churches and six Roman Catholic churches in different parts of the country suggest that congregations closely resemble their counterparts in most present-day Anglican churches, in size, age-group, and ratio of the sexes. There is at the moment a delicate balance between Church and State in Yugoslavia—but it is a balance which might easily be lost if one of the Churches became associated with any political group hostile to the existing way of life.

In 1950 the best-known political prisoner in Yugoslavia was Archbishop Stepinac; twelve years later, ironically enough, it was one of the leaders of the Government which had imprisoned him, Milovan Djilas. When, on the last day of 1962, *The Times* of London published its annual retrospect of the previous twelve months, the only Yugoslav whom it mentioned was

Djilas; and this is typical of the interest which his case has aroused outside his own country in recent years.

Milovan Djilas was born in Montenegro in 1912, the son of a peasant. He became a communist while still a schoolboy and at the University of Belgrade in the early nineteen-thirties emerged as the leader of a group of singularly rebellious students. He was arrested and imprisoned by the royal authorities in 1933. By 1941 he was accepted as one of the finest brains in the Party. He distinguished himself with the Partisans in his native Montenegro and in Bosnia as a ruthless and dedicated fighter, and was sent to Moscow as one of the first Yugoslav communist representatives in 1944. From 1945 to 1953 he was in the inner circle of communist leaders, taking a strongly anti-Stalinist line in the dispute of 1948 and becoming one of the Vice-Presidents. But Djilas remained a strong idealist. He was shocked by the way in which Party leaders acquired cars and luxury flats once they had come to power; they were hardly distinguishable, he felt, from the despised politicians of the inter-war years.

In the light of this experience, Djilas began to re-examine his Marxist convictions and to express thoughts which were markedly different from those of his colleagues. British Labour leaders found Djilas openly favouring the substitution of political democracy for the one-party dictatorship of communist doctrine. And Djilas was too much of a Martin Luther to keep his views for the privacy of after-dinner conversation. They began to slip into articles which he wrote for the leading Party newspaper, *Borba*, and they dominated an intellectual magazine which he edited, a kind of Yugoslav *New Statesman* called *Nova Misao* ('New Thought'). Political leaders, particularly those concerned with internal security, disliked these sniping attacks on their new careers from a trenchant writer. For a time his close friendship with Tito protected Djilas; but he made many enemies. In 1954 he was expelled from the League of Communists and dismissed from his posts in the Government. Twice he was put on trial in 1955-56 but received what were, in effect, cautionary sentences. Undaunted, he persisted in his criticisms and a frank interview which he gave to an American newspaperman in 1957 led, once more, to his arrest. This time he was sentenced to seven years imprisonment and taken off to the jail at Sremska Mitrovica where he had served his term in the nineteen-thirties.

While Djilas was in prison, a manuscript which he had written before his arrest was published in Britain, Germany, and the U.S.A. as a book entitled *The New Class*. Although difficult to read and understand, it remains one of the most important contributions to communist theory in the last thirty years. For Djilas, while accepting all the conventional Marxist views of the inevitability of revolution in backward and exploited lands, maintained that these revolutions, instead of abolishing class distinctions, merely substituted the rule of a new group of successful communist leaders for the rule of the old privileged capitalists. Such an analysis was in itself a dangerous doctrine in a communist state; but Djilas went even further, and predicted that the dictatorship of the New Class carried with it the seeds of its own destruction, either in the form of divisions among rival communist states or as a second rising of the down-trodden masses. Djilas's views were taken up and exploited by groups outside Yugoslavia who had nothing but hatred for socialist ideals, in the ultimate success of which Djilas had shown he remained a fervent believer. However much Western liberals deplored his arrest, it is small wonder that the Yugoslav authorities kept him in prison, nor can Djilas have been surprised at his own fate. He was years ahead of the political thaw. In other communist countries he could hardly have kept his life, let alone his liberty.

After serving nearly four years of his imprisonment, Djilas was released on the understanding that he refrained from anti-communist attacks in foreign periodicals. But Djilas was too courageous to be silenced. Early in 1962 an Italian magazine carried a short story (later printed in *Encounter*) in which he depicted the bestiality of all war, even the type of fighting ennobled by devotion to the Partisan cause. A few weeks later it was announced in America that Djilas had sent a further manuscript to be published abroad, *Conversations with Stalin*, an account of his meetings with Soviet leaders during and immediately after the Second World War. On April 8th, 1962, he was arrested yet again; five weeks later, after a secret trial, he was sent back to prison for five years and the residue of his previous sentence. The Yugoslav authorities emphasized that Djilas had revealed state secrets in his book (although it contains few facts not already known). It is, of course, true that for this offence he would have received a prison sentence in Britain, the U.S.A., or Germany no less than in Yugoslavia. Whether this is the end of his political career remains to be seen. There have been other communist states in which disgraced leaders have emerged from prison to lead their country along the course to which they have remained personally loyal. Most Yugoslavs today prefer to maintain an embarrassed silence on the Djilas Affair; and yet, whatever its outcome, the man himself seems assured of a place in history—for even those who do not agree with his views must surely respect his characteristically Montenegrin courage.

The re-arrest of Djilas in April 1962 surprised some foreign observers because it ran counter to a tendency towards greater personal freedom which had been shown in several ways in previous months. Only a fortnight before, a thousand political prisoners had been pardoned as part of a general amnesty, which also removed penalties imposed on 150,000 people who had fled from the country during and after the war, and who might now return, if they wished, as free citizens. At the same time irksome visa formalities were reduced for visiting tourists and the Yugoslavs themselves were given easier facilities for obtaining passports to go abroad. Since, however, they could only take a small sum of money out of the country with them, less than 300,000 people were able to take advantage of this concession in the course of the year.

In retrospect, there seems little doubt that the timing of Djilas's arrest was connected, not with home affairs, but with a major re-adjustment of Yugoslav foreign policy that became clear in the second half of 1962. To understand these developments we must at this point interrupt our narrative and examine the basis of Yugoslavia's attitude towards international affairs.

Yugoslav foreign policy in the last ten years has rested on three assumptions, all of which we have touched upon already in this book. The first of these assumptions is ideological: the belief that it is essential for a country to tread its own 'road to socialism', independent of both the communist tradition of the East and the social democratic tradition of the West. The second assumption is economic: that Yugoslavia needs to buy and to sell in free competition in all parts of the world and especially in the underdeveloped areas. The third assumption is strategic: that a major European war (even one fought with 'conventional' weapons) would be disastrous for Yugoslavia, since if she were involved in it she could hardly hope to safeguard her long and vulnerable frontiers from invasion, and if she were not involved— an improbable condition, sandwiched as she is between seven different states—she would be cut off from essential markets and ultimately menaced by any power bloc strong enough to emerge victorious. These three assumptions have accordingly dictated a policy of neutrality, independence, and peaceful co-operation. The fundamental principles of foreign policy are stated in the preface to the new Constitution, which formally records adherence to the international commitments implied through membership of the United Nations. Nevertheless, while there is no reason for supposing that Yugoslavia will abandon her principles in the foreseeable future, there are outside circumstances which appear to be forcing President Tito to modify their application in certain respects. This is shown most clearly in the Yugoslav attitude to the Soviet Union.

Relations between the Soviet Union and Yugoslavia since 1955 have shown all the breath-taking variations in temperament of a 'teen-age romance. There have been reconciliations and gifts and rows and flirting with that Common Market boy next door and more reconciliations, more gifts, more angry words, and further covert glances across the garden-fence; and so on. For most of 1956 and much of 1957 contact between Moscow and Belgrade was particularly close, until Tito refused to associate himself with a resolution on Marxist doctrine made by all the communist parties celebrating the fortieth anniversary of the Bolshevik Revolution. Then it became clear that the Russians were no more prepared to accept an independently minded communist in 1957 than they had been in 1948. The feud was renewed: the Russians surpassed themselves in references to the loyalty of the Albanian comrades; the Yugoslavs negotiated trade-agreements with Italy; and in 1960, eighty-one communist parties meeting in Moscow solemnly condemned Tito for having betrayed the Marxist cause. In July 1961 the Yugoslav Foreign Minister was welcomed in Moscow with friendly articles in the Press; two months later he was attacked in the same newspapers for 'slanderously resorting to the basest libels about the Soviet Union'. Then in April 1962 (just after the unfortunate Djilas had been re-arrested) the Soviet Foreign Minister came to Belgrade for talks. In September the Soviet President paid a state visit to Yugoslavia. In December President Tito went to Russia, and returned 'with much greater optimism', asking the rhetorical question, 'Why should we have worse relations with socialist countries than we have with some Western countries?' It was assumed that the Yugoslav and Russian communist parties would shortly re-establish the 'fraternal relations' broken off in 1948, but that Tito had impressed on Khrushchev his determination to remain outside the Russian-dominated Warsaw Pact.

There are some grounds for believing that this new friendship between Russia and Yugoslavia will endure, even though earlier reconciliations were almost ludicrously brief. Conditions have changed; the Russians can no longer rely on other communist parties dutifully following their lead. There is, as it were, a rival Pope in Peking to challenge the infallibility of the Kremlin. The Chinese communists roundly condemn everything Yugoslav. The basis of their hostility is outwardly ideological, a dispute over the true character of socialism, but behind all the reams of Marxist jargon lies old-fashioned and discredited political rivalry. This is no academic squabble between countries thousands of miles apart. Genuine interests are at stake.

Ever since 1950, when the Yugoslavs were hosts to an unofficial Peace Congress in Zagreb, they have prided themselves on their connections with other neutral states. These contacts have won them prestige; more practically, they have brought trade links. And one of the regions in the world where Yugoslavia has had greatest influence has been in South-East Asia, particularly in India and Indonesia, territories on China's doorstep, where men with socialist inclinations might have been expected to turn respectfully towards Peking. The Chinese took the Yugoslav threat so seriously that early in 1961 they began to lavish support on Albania, that tiny communist republic isolated from the Soviet-dominated countries and peopled by a million and a half 'Shqiptars', of the same race as 800,000 Yugoslav citizens in neighbouring Kosmet and Macedonia. This was a challenge that Tito could not ignore. But neither could Khrushchev; for if the Chinese were allowed to cultivate a European state with whom the Russians had a military alliance, then Russia might find herself pitched into a war which she did not desire on the initiative of Peking. Khrushchev determined to make a stand, indirectly against the Chinese, openly against the wretched Albanians. In October 1961 the Albanians were accused of 'Stalinism', all Russian aid was withdrawn, and diplomatic relations between Russia and Albania were broken off (a breach greater even than that with Yugoslavia in 1948). And so long as Khrushchev continues to denounce the Stalinists in Albania, he may be sure of support from the oldest anti-Stalinist of all in the communist world, President Tito.

Apart from the distant abuse of the Chinese and the more immediate pin-prick from Albania, the Yugoslavs had two reasons of their own for seeking to improve relations with the Soviet Union; one of these is economic, the other political. In Chapter Three we noticed the way in which trade between Russia and Yugoslavia has increased proportionately with the growth of the European Economic Community. The Yugoslavs want, if possible, to have the best of both commercial worlds: they would welcome the chance to send observers to Brussels to keep in touch with the Common Market countries; but they also wish to send observers to Moscow, so that they can negotiate with its Russian-sponsored rival, Comecon. Since there are political undertones about both the E.E.C. and Comecon, they consider that, of the two, there is more likelihood of their securing favourable terms from the other communist states; although, as we have seen, they have reservations about the value and character of trade with the Soviet Union.

The political motive behind the act of reconciliation is both curious and devious. In September 1961 a Conference of the Heads of State of Non-Aligned Countries was held in Belgrade. The Emperor of Ethiopia, the President of the United Arab Republic, the President of Ghana, the President of the Indonesian Republic, the Indian Prime Minister, and a score of other dignitaries from Asia and Africa gathered in the Yugoslav capital. The Conference took place at a time of considerable international tension. A separatist movement in the Congo province of Katanga, backed by European mercenaries, was defying resolutions of the United Nations.

And a fortnight before the Conference opened the communist authorities of East Berlin had erected a wall bisecting the occupied city. As if this were not enough, on the very eve of the Conference the Russians announced that they were resuming nuclear testing in the atmosphere. The Western Powers expected the Conference to condemn the Russian actions. Twenty-four of the nations represented in Belgrade (including Yugoslavia) had received in recent years five million pounds of aid from the United States. Lest the Conference should be unaware of what he considered its duty, President Kennedy sent a message to Belgrade making his views on the Russian announcement abundantly clear. The message was duly read out to the Conference, there were gestures of carefully non-aligned agreement from the delegates—but the Conference did not single out the Russians for attack. The Uncommitted Countries remained solidly uncommitted. They announced their intention of persisting in working for a relaxation of world-tension through the United Nations; and, after a week of public debate, they adjourned.

The United States considered that the Belgrade Conference had achieved nothing, a view which the Yugoslavs maintained would be refuted in the United Nations Assembly. The Americans were angry, understandably from their point of view. The U.S. attitude towards Yugoslavia began to harden. Senator Fulbright, an influential spokesman on foreign affairs, declared, 'We must not be blackmailed into providing lavish aid'. The Internal Security Subcommittee of the United States Senate asked for a report on Yugoslav communism; it was submitted five weeks after the Belgrade Conference broke up and was prepared by a pre-war Yugoslav diplomat in exile. While admitting distinctions between the

Yugoslav and Soviet brands of communism, it was fundamentally hostile; Tito's neutralism was branded as 'a tactic for spreading communist ideas to other countries'. The effect of the report was soon felt elsewhere. An important group in Congress sought to terminate the arrangements under which the Yugoslavs received favourable trade-terms in the U.S.A. Relations between the two countries deteriorated to a lower level than at any time since 1948; and, inevitably, the Yugoslavs sought to insure themselves elsewhere.

The Belgrade Conference caused heart-searching in Peking and Moscow no less than in Washington. The Chinese felt affronted. Six years earlier they had dominated an Afro-Asian Conference at Bandung; now they were excluded and their place taken by the Yugoslavs. The Russian attitude towards a gathering of neutrals under Tito's chairmanship was at first as cold as the Chinese. American indignation made them re-assess their position. Khrushchev began to see that Yugoslavia could provide him with a bridge which would enable him to show the Afro-Asian neutrals that friendship with Russia did not mean absorption. Even in 1955 he had been prepared to agree on paper with the Yugoslavs that there might be 'different roads to socialism'; now he was willing to make a genuine acceptance of what had hitherto been little more than theory. Hence the visits of the Soviet Foreign Minister and President to Belgrade (when the Yugoslavs were embarrassed by the violently anti-American speeches of their guest) and Tito's conversations with Khrushchev in Moscow.

Nearly nine hundred years ago the German Emperor Henry IV tried to defy the Papacy, failed, crossed into Italy and humbled himself barefooted in the snow before the Pope in the town of Canossa. Rightly or wrongly, this act has remained over the centuries a symbol of humiliating surrender. Tito's journey through the mid-winter snow to Moscow was no Canossa. He went as a man with special status among the new nations of the world. He was not asking to be received back into the fold. Although Khrushchev would have welcomed a military alliance, Tito remained independent. 'There are still matters on which we do not agree, though we admit that these will be eliminated by practice, without compulsion,' said the President on his return to Belgrade. So far from accepting Moscow's direction, Tito still hopes that other states (and particularly Hungary and Poland) will secure the freedom of movement upon which he has insisted for Yugoslavia. Some commentators have thought that this hope is unrealistic—but then was it realistic to break with Stalin in 1948?

President Tito's personal prestige at home and abroad remains as high as it has ever been. The revolutionary has assumed the mantle of an elder statesman; he has become a legend in his own lifetime. This is, perhaps, a mixed blessing. Living legends tend later to become liabilities; they rarely make easier the task of their successors, as Richard Cromwell found in seventeenth-century England. President Tito, who celebrated his seventieth birthday in May 1962, appears to appreciate this problem and is gradually bringing the other Yugoslav leaders more and more into the public eye. It is time for us to look at the men around him.

For more than twenty years Tito's right-hand man has been Edvard Kardelj. In 1953 he became the senior Vice-President, and he has already been mentioned in this chapter as the head of the commission which prepared the new Constitution. Kardelj is a Slovene, born into a working-class family in Ljubljana in 1910. A stockily-built man, with hair brushed straight back and a small black moustache, he leans forward to peer earnestly through almost rimless spectacles. When he addresses an assembly, there is no political playing to the gallery; he lectures, with all the dry reliability of an orthodox schoolmaster. And that, indeed, is the profession he should have followed, for he was trained as a teacher at Ljubljana University. He became a communist while at school and his undergraduate radical views soon attracted the attention of police spies. He was arrested and so badly tortured that he was left with a permanent limp. His political record made it impossible for him to teach and he escaped across the frontier, travelling first to France and then to Russia. By 1937, when Tito began to re-organize the Communist Party, Kardelj was accepted as one of the ablest commentators on doctrine and he returned to Yugoslavia, secretly joining Tito in Zagreb.

In the summer of 1941 Kardelj was despatched to Slovenia to plan resistance against the Germans and Italians. He was with Tito in some of the earliest fighting of the Partisan War but then, disguised as a railway fireman, ran the gauntlet of German guard posts to travel three hundred miles with instructions for the Slovene communists. For eighteen months he directed their operations from a closely guarded cellar in his native city, linked by a radio transmitter with Tito's headquarters. But when German parachutists nearly captured Tito at Drvar in 1944, Kardelj was there once again and was subsequently sent with Djilas to head the first diplomatic mission to Stalin. He seems to have struck the Russians as far too astute and independent, for in 1948 he was one of the Yugoslav leaders singled out for particular condemnation. Since 1948 Kardelj has been so pre-occupied with the evolution of constitutional law that he has taken little part in international affairs, although he has been on a private visit to London. He has never captured the public imagination, but, for many years, he seemed a likely successor to President Tito.

Yet in July 1963 it was announced that Tito's deputy would be not Kardelj, but the former second Vice-President, Aleksandar Ranković. Born in 1909 in the Šumadija, the very heart of Serbia, he was apprenticed as a tailor, became a communist agitator in 1927, was captured and badly beaten up, served six years in prison and, like Kardelj, was closely associated with Tito's re-organization of the Party in 1937. In July 1942 Ranković was arrested by the Gestapo (the German secret police) after a gun-battle in Belgrade in which he was wounded. Two days after his capture he was rescued from hospital in a daring raid by some forty communists, who smuggled him out of the city hidden in a bullock cart. He served at Tito's headquarters throughout the Partisan War, supervising Party organization and intelligence work. In 1945 he became Minister of the Interior, in charge of the secret police, with the immediate task of eliminating political opponents and capturing Mihailović. Ranković continued to be especially responsible for internal security as Vice-President. It is reasonable to assume that the senior posts in the police force and militia have been filled by his nominees ever since the establishment of the Republic, although for the last ten years they have been nominally under the direction of his successor as Minister of the Interior, Sveteslav Stefanović. Ranković and Stefanović, his junior in age by a few months, have had their careers linked closely together for more than thirty years. Both came from the Serbian peasantry, both joined the communist youth movement in 1927 and the Party a year later. They served prison sentences together, they co-operated in the war (which both ended with the rank of General), and they ran the State Security Police together. There seems every probability that this partnership will continue.

Ranković is a heavily-built man, with greying hair, a firm mouth and chin, and hard eyes which look small set between prominent Slavic cheek-bones. He has never been one of the intellectuals of the communist movement, but he wields considerable authority on the executive of the Socialist Alliance. Only rarely does he intervene in foreign affairs, and when he does so it is with Yugoslavia's immediate neighbours. Thus he headed an important delegation to Athens in 1961, and was sent to Rome in June 1962 to sound out the Italians during the reconciliation with Russia. He is probably the most powerful man in the League of Communists. Much of the future of Yugoslavia rests on his ability to continue working together with Kardelj, who is in many ways his opposite in character and personality.

Neither of the other two Vice-Presidents exercised as much influence as Kardelj and Ranković. Rodoljub Colaković is a Bosnian, nine years older than Ranković. He was a schoolboy in Sarajevo when many of his elder schoolfellows were involved in the ' Young Bosnia ' movement, which played a prominent part in the assassination of the Austrian Archduke in 1914. A Communist Party member in 1919, Colaković served a ten-year prison sentence before escaping across the frontier and fighting in the International Brigade in the Spanish Civil War. In 1941 he organized resistance in Bosnia-Herzegovina. As Vice-President his particular responsibility was education. Mijalko Todorović was the youngest of the Vice-Presidents. Born in 1913, the son of a Serbian peasant, he did not become a Party member until 1938. His particular interest is agriculture; he is said to favour closer economic collaboration with Russia.

The most interesting figure among the communist leaders is probably Koča Popović, the dapper elegantly dressed Foreign Minister with a Hollywood profile. Ever since the establishment of the Republic he has been in the forefront of international affairs and for most of this period he has headed the Yugoslav Foreign Office. He has thus been Tito's principal partner in the delicate balancing-act of the last fifteen years. Popović was born in Belgrade in 1908, the son of an extremely wealthy businessman. He became a communist while a student at Belgrade University; so too did two other members of the Popović family who have subsequently held high office. He left Yugoslavia to study in Paris, but went to Spain and fought in the International Brigade. When he joined the Partisans in 1941 he had the rare distinction of being not only a veteran soldier, but also an able student of law, an abstract artist, and a poet. He fought as a Corps Commander throughout the Partisan War, which he ended as a full General. For some years after the war he was Chief of the General Staff, but his knowledge of foreign conditions made him an invaluable adviser on international problems. He has headed missions to many parts of the world as well as accompanying Tito on most of his foreign journeys, including the visit to London in 1953.

In July 1963 the Federal Council approved the appointment of Petar Stambolić as the first prime minister under the new Constitutional Law. This was, in some ways, an unexpected choice since he had been out of the forefront of politics for the previous six years as

'Speaker' of the Yugoslav parliament. Born in 1912 in a Serbian village, Stambolić studied the economic structure of rural communities at Belgrade University in the fiery 'thirties, organized partisan resistance in eastern Serbia in 1941, and, with the backing of Ranković, became after the war an influential political figure within the Serbian Republic, of which he was premier from 1952 to 1957. It remains to be seen whether, as 'President of the Federal Executive Council', Stambolić will lead the government, or, as his career would seem to indicate, be content to act as an administrative chairman, with real authority remaining in the hands of President Tito or his deputy, Vice-President Ranković.

Many communists prominent in setting up the Republic have now disappeared from the scene. Some are dead, Moša Pijade, the brilliant Jewish intellectual, and Boris Kidrić, the creator of the Workers' Councils; among them. Others are out of favour. Meanwhile new political figures are coming to the fore. At the Belgrade Conference of 1961 the burden of the secretarial work was entrusted to a fifty-year-old Croatian lawyer, Leo Mates, who had been a highly successful Ambassador to the U.S.A. And when, five months later, relations between France and Yugoslavia were strained because of Yugoslav sympathy for the Algerian nationalists, Mates was hastily sent to Paris with the unenviable task of soothing the ruffled feelings of President de Gaulle. Mates, a slightly-built man who speaks fluent English with hardly a trace of accent, is at present Assistant Secretary for Foreign Affairs and may take a leading role in shaping Yugoslav foreign policy in the next decade. So too may the head of the Committee for Foreign Trade, Sergej Krajger, the forty-eight-year-old Slovene economist who in the second half of 1962 conducted delicate negotiations with both the E.E.C. and Comecon. Finally, among Party leaders there is Miko Tripalo, the administrative head of the People's Youth Organization, an energetic young Croat who enlisted in the Partisans in 1941 at the age of fifteen and was demobilized as a war-hardened captain of nineteen to become a student at Zagreb University. At present Tripalo is striving to awaken the political consciousness of the younger generation. He holds a post of great importance for the future.

Yugoslavia, it must be remembered, is not only a young country in order of years; it is also a land in which young people constitute a larger proportion of the population than in most states that have had a longer existence. More than half of the eighteen and a half million Yugoslavs are under the age of twenty-five; the same age-group in Britain comprises slightly over a third of the population. Indeed, there is as high a proportion of Yugoslavs under twenty-five as there is of British under thirty-six. The youth of Yugoslavia have contributed much to the constructive work of the last eighteen years, but their relative numerical preponderance is of greater political significance than any co-operative projects that they have already accomplished. For they hold the keys of tomorrow. If they are contented, the Yugoslav Federation will flourish; if they are not, it could disintegrate.

There are no Gallup Polls in communist states and it is notoriously difficult to assess public opinion. From time to time there seems evidence of unrest. Thus there were disturbances in the universities of Skopje and Zagreb in the course of 1959, and in December 1962 some Slovenes were sentenced in Ljubljana for membership of a terrorist organization which, it was alleged, was directed by exiles in Western Germany. Reports of trouble tend, however, to be over-dramatized. There is certainly some inter-republican sensitivity—Slovenes and Croats feel that they carry the backward South on their backs—but nothing to resemble the national antagonisms of the inter-war period. Then, travellers noted that talk in the cafés was of politics, of the trickery of Serb or Croat or both; now, as like as not, it is of pop-music or fashions and, above all, of sport. A Yugoslav city on the eve of a football match between two leading teams has all the excited tumult of London's West End when a Northern side comes 'up for Cup'; and, after all, the Yugoslavs did finish fourth in the 1962 World Tournament in Chile.

Perhaps the younger generation is politically apathetic. Veteran communists have often expressed alarm at its apparent frivolity. But is not this a sign of acceptance of the present order, a sign of national maturity? The Revolution is beginning to recede. A young Serb who was twenty-five in 1963 was only six years old when the Germans were driven out of Belgrade in October 1944. He may have horrific memories of the war years, but he will have known no other Yugoslav leader than Tito and no other system of government than the present Federation. And this already applies to half the population. The Yugoslav peoples in general have had greater stability of government and greater prosperity in the years in which this generation has reached manhood than ever before. Their system is not for export to Britain or the U.S.A., and this is not their concern. They accept the need for changes from time to time— as the recent constitutional discussions have shown— but they have no wish to destroy the basic structure of the state: why should they?

# SUGGESTIONS FOR FURTHER READING

## FACTUAL

DRAGUTIN SUBOTIĆ, *Yugoslav Popular Ballads; Their Origin and Development* (C. U. P., 1935). A valuable and stimulating introduction to the subject.

REBECCA WEST, *Black Lamb and Grey Falcon* (Macmillan, 1942). Ostensibly an account of a journey to Yugoslavia in 1937, but written with such depth of feeling that it becomes something greater, even for those who may not share all of Dame Rebecca's enthusiasms. A classic of its kind.

R. J. KERNER (ed.), *Yugoslavia* (Berkeley, California, 1949). A useful collection of studies on many topics.

STEPHEN CLISSOLD, *Whirlwind* (Cresset Press, 1949). A judicious study of the divided loyalties in occupied Yugoslavia.

FITZROY MACLEAN, *Eastern Approaches* (Jonathan Cape, 1949). A splendidly written account of his experiences, by the head of the British wartime mission to Tito. (Paperback edition by Pan Books, 1956).

H. SETON-WATSON, *The East European Revolution* (Methuen, 1950). Analytical narrative of events in Yugoslavia and her neighbours, 1941-49.

VLADIMIR DEDIJER. *Tito Speaks* (Weidenfeld & Nicolson, 1953). The authorized biography, narrated by a distinguished historian.

FITZROY MACLEAN, *Disputed Barricade* (Jonathan Cape, 1957). A first-rate biography of Tito which portrays him against the background of the Yugoslav Revolution.

MILOVAN DJILAS, *Land without Justice* (Methuen, 1958). A delightfully written autobiographical study of Montenegro nearly fifty years ago.

ERNST HALPERIN, *The Triumphant Heretic* (Heinemann, 1958). A critical assessment of Yugoslav developments between 1945 and 1956 by an able Swiss journalist.

MURIEL HEPPELL AND F. H. SINGLETON, *Yugoslavia* (Benn, 1961). A convenient historical survey, better on mediaeval times than later on.

VLADIMIR DEDIJER, *The Beloved Land* (MacGibbon and Kee, 1961). A moving autobiography by a former colonel with the Partisans in Bosnia.

C. A. MACARTNEY AND A. W. PALMER, *Independent Eastern Europe* (Macmillan, 1962). Primarily a history of the years 1914-41. It includes sections on the formation, evolution, and dissolution of the First Yugoslavia, and has an extensive reading-list and maps.

RODOLJUB COLAKOVIĆ, *Winning Freedom* (Lincolns-Prager, 1962). A shortened version of the War Memoirs of a man who was later to become one of the Vice-Presidents; particularly interesting on the Jajce A.V.N.O.J. Congress of 1943.

PHYLLIS AUTY, *Yugoslavia* (Weidenfeld & Nicolson, 1962). This is mainly a travel book for the 'Young Explorer', but it contains a great deal of interesting material and is pleasant reading.

### FICTION

The two most famous novels of the first Yugoslav Nobel Prize winner may be recommended: Ivo ANDRIĆ, *Bosnian Story* and *The Bridge over the Drina*.

# SOME DATES IN THE HISTORY
# OF THE SOUTH SLAVS

A.D.

*c.* 586-626   Arrival of Slav groups in the area of present-day Yugoslavia

1102   Koloman of Hungary becomes King of Croatia

1168-96   Stephen Nemanya builds up mediaeval Serbian Kingdom

1331-55   Reign of Stephen Dušan, King of Serbia

1389   28th June: Battle of Kosovo; Serbs overwhelmed by Turks

1527   Croats accept Ferdinand of Habsburg (Emperor) as King

1804-13   Revolt of Karadjordje Petrović in Serbia

1815-17   Revolt of Miloš Obrenović in Serbia

1817-39   Miloš reigns as first hereditary Prince of Serbia

1867   'Compromise', creating Austria-Hungary, leaves Croatia within Hungarian Kingdom

1878   March: Treaty of San Stefano formally recognizes Serbian independence

July: Treaty of Berlin authorizes Austria-Hungary to occupy Bosnia-Herzegovina

1903   Serbs overthrow Obrenović dynasty; Peter Karadjordjević King

1908   'Bosnian Crisis', caused by Austro-Hungarian annexation of Bosnia-Herzegovina

1912-13   Balkan Wars lead to doubling in size of Serbia and Montenegro

1914   28th June: Assassination of Archduke Francis Ferdinand at Sarajevo

28th July: Austria-Hungary declares war on Serbia; start of First World War

1915 (Oct.)-1916 (Jan.)  Retreat of Serbs through Serbia and Albania

1917  20th July: Corfu Pact provides for setting up Yugoslav Kingdom after the war

1918  1st Dec.: Formal proclamation of 'Kingdom of Serbs, Croats, and Slovenes'

1929  6th Jan.: King Alexander establishes royal dictatorship in Yugoslavia

1934  9th Oct.: King Alexander assassinated at Marseilles

1941  27th March: Anti-German *coup d'état* in Belgrade

6th April: Yugoslavia invaded by the Axis Powers; mass-bombing of Belgrade

7th July: Partisan War begins in Serbia

1943  29th Nov.: Second A.V.N.O.J. Congress at Jajce demands federal republic

1945  29th Nov.: Yugoslavia proclaimed a Federal People's Republic

1948  28th June: Yugoslavia expelled from 'family of fraternal Communist Parties'

1953  January: Marshal Tito elected President

1961  Sept.: Belgrade Conference of 'Uncommitted Nations'

1963  April: Acceptance of new constitutional law by Federal Assembly

# INDEX

# INDEX

Italy, 25, 39, 40-41, 43, 44, 46, 55

Jajce, 54, 56
Jesenice, 7, 23, 70

Karadjordje ('Black George'), 22, 31, 32, 36
Kardelj, E., 75, 92, 93, 96, 97, 98, 114-16, 117
Khrushchev, N., 51, 61, 109, 110, 113, 114
Kidrić, B., 76, 119
Kosmet, 13, 110
Kosovo, 30, 32, 36, 37
Kragujevac, 16
Krajger, S., 119, 120

Ljubljana, 9, 10, 115

Macedonia, 9, 11, 18, 28, 29
Maclean, Brigadier F., 54
Maize, 67, 83
Mates, L., 119
Mestrović, I., 11
Metternich, C., 33, 34
Mihailović D., 49, 55, 56, 57, 116
Military Frontier, 32, 33
Mineral Resources, 12, 23, 70
Montenegro, 11, 12, 17, 19, 35, 36, 40, 48, 72
Morava, 64, 65
Muslims, 9, 30, 100-1, 103
Mussolini, B., 43

NATO, 25
Nemanyid Dynasty, 29
Nikita, King, 36, 40
Njegoš, P. P., Prince-Bishop, 19

Obradović, D., 19
Obrenović Dynasty, 32, 36
Oil, 70, 71
Orthodox Church, 9, 31, 100-3

Partisans, 49, 52-53, 54, 55, 101
Pašić, N., 36, 38, 41, 42, 49
Paul, Prince, 45, 46, 47
Pavelić, A., 48, 58
Peoples Youth Organization, 99, 120
Peter I, King, 36, 41
Peter II, King, 22, 44, 47, 48, 55, 56
Pigs, 68
Pijade, M., 119
Popović, K., 118
Population, 15, 20, 79, 80, 120
Princip, G., 37
Pula, 27, 71

Railways, 21, 63, 65, 66
Ranković, A., 116-17
Rashka, 29
Ribar, President I., 54, 56
Rijeka (Fiume), 41, 71
Roads, 24, 63, 66, 69
Roman Catholicism, 9, 34, 57-59, 100-3
Roumania, 26, 35
Russia (U.S.S.R.), 14, 35, 51, 53, 56, 59, 60, 61, 73, 81, 85, 96, 108-9

Salonika, 38, 65
San Stefano, Treaty, 35
Sarajevo, 9, 37, 50, 67, 117
Sava, 9, 64, 65
Seper, Monsignor, 59, 102
Serbia, 9, 12, 13, 14, 15, 17, 21, 29, 31, 32, 35, 39, 42, 43, 48, 49, 53, 68, 116
Serbo-Croat, 17
Shipbuilding, 71
Simović, General D., 47
Skopje, 9, 29, 36, 67, 103
*Sljivovica*, 67
Slovenia, 10, 18, 19, 28, 52, 68, 72, 115
Socialist Alliance, 99, 117

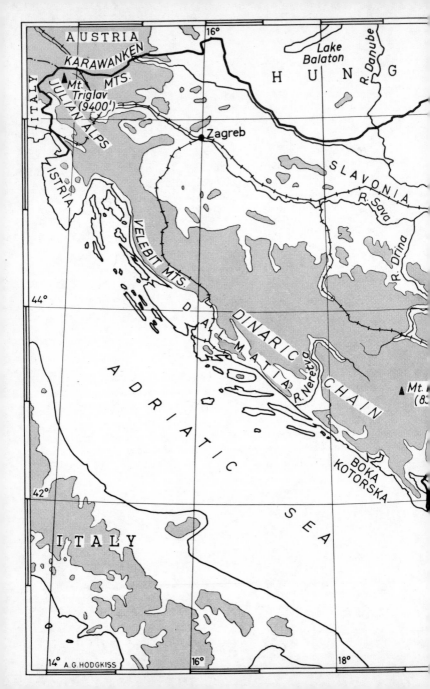